# FOREWORD

This workbook should prove an invaluable aid for teachers, parents and students. It is the word bank companion to 'Writing with Stardust'. Each of the 20 chapters has a fill in the blanks spelling section. This will enable any student to improve their spellings and their thought patterns at the same time.

It also has advice for educators on how to use 'Writing with Stardust' to maximum benefit. From explaining how to write a diary to teaching students how to think, this is the definitive descriptive writing workbook. It will improve a student's knowledge base, diction, planning skills and self-confidence. It even shows how to break down and grade an essay into twenty separate parts. By the time this workbook is completed, any student will find that their writing has been transformed.

It is designed to be parent and teacher friendly. If you want to combine eunoia (beautiful thinking) with writing with stardust, this is the workbook to purchase.

Blog @ www.descriptivewriting.wordpress.com

Accompanying video on YouTube entitled Writing with Stardust

Email Liam at oflynn.liam42@gmail.com

# TABLE OF CONTENTS

# RIVERS AND STREAMS

## COLOUR

| 1 point | 2 points | 3 points | 4 points | 5 points | TOTAL |
|---|---|---|---|---|---|
| cr_sta_ - blue | sap_hi_e- blue | g_mst__e- blue | bu__e_fl_ - blue | d__g_nf__ - blue | |
| je_e_ - blue | g_m-blue | turq_io_e- blue | d_c_ eg_ - blue | k__gf_s_e_ - blue | |

### MAKE A SENTENCE

1.

2.

## SOUND

| | | | | | TOTAL |
|---|---|---|---|---|---|
| spl__h_ng | o_z_ng | bab__ing | m_rm_ring | pu__ing | |
| tric__ing | se_p_ng | bur__ing | thr_m_ing | pu_ing | |

### MAKE A SENTENCE

1.

2.

## SHAPE

| | | | | | TOTAL |
|---|---|---|---|---|---|
| tw_s_ed | sw__ved | wo__d | sn__ed | me__de_er | |
| cu_ved | co__ed | w_aved | zi_za__ed | wen_ed | |

### MAKE A SENTENCE

1.

2.

## ACTION

| | | | | | TOTAL |
|---|---|---|---|---|---|
| hop_ed | ju__ed | spr__g | hu_dled | bo_n_ed | |
| sk__ped | le_ped | d_n_ed | va_l_ed | ji__ed | |

### MAKE A SENTENCE

1.

2.

## METAPHORS FOR RIVERS                    TOTAL

| | | | | | |
|---|---|---|---|---|---|
| roa_s | ve_ns | liq__d soul | li_e_lood | pla__a | |
| moto_w_ys | art__ies | pum_ing soul | li_u_d sp_r_t | eli__r | |

## MAKE A SENTENCE

1.

2.

## WATER REFLECTING                    TOTAL

| | | | | | |
|---|---|---|---|---|---|
| flas__ing | sp__k_ing | glo__ng | gl__ting | gli_t_ng | |
| fl__k_ring | shi__er_ng | gl__ming | gl__e__ng | gli__m__ing | |

## MAKE A SENTENCE

1.

2.

## OTHER IMAGES                    TOTAL

| | | | | | |
|---|---|---|---|---|---|
| swans gli_ing | pebbles tum__ing | trou_ slo_hing | t__gs tw__ing | wh___po__s wh__ing | |
| ducks pad__ing | bu__er_lies flu__ring | drag____ies wh__z__g | __gfi___rs fi__ing | __she_m_n's li__hi__ng | |

## MAKE A SENTENCE

1.

2.

## SENSATION

| 2 points | 3 points | 5 points | TOTAL |
|---|---|---|---|
| refre__ing | stim__ating | thirst-quen__ing | |
| ener__sing | invigo___ing | thirst-sla__ng | |

## MAKE A SENTENCE

1.

2.

### SMELL                    TOTAL

| sc_nt | fra_ra_e | per_me | |
| a_oma | wa_t | colo_e | |

## MAKE A SENTENCE

1.

2.

### TASTE                    TOTAL

| yu__y | lu_h | scru_ti_us | |
| ri_h | del_i_us | subl_e | |

## MAKE A SENTENCE

1.

2.

# PLANNING A PARAGRAPH

The purpose of this grid system is to plan a paragraph on the 'Rivers and Streams' chapter. The concept is very simple. The students should be encouraged to paint in a scene using their 'artist's eye'. This means that they should be dividing up a scene like this into its different components.

Each student should be encouraged to memorise one word in each grid which matches their level. One point can be awarded for each word they fill in. If they get 9 points or more, they should get a reward. The process can then be repeated for the second word in their grid. Underneath the grids, there are fifteen sentences. The student should be encouraged to sketch in five more details to the passage. After every two sentences using the grids, an original sentence of their own should be added. It could be a bird in the sky, other characters by the river or different colours and sounds. After this, the lines should be rewritten in three paragraphs of five sentences each. The exercise may then be checked for spellings, syntax and errors of punctuation and grammar.

| COLOUR | SHAPE | METAPHORS | IMAGES | SMELL |
|---|---|---|---|---|
| | | | | |
| SOUND | ACTION | REFLECTING | SENSATION | TASTE |
| | | | | |

| COLOUR | SHAPE | METAPHORS | IMAGES | SMELL |
|---|---|---|---|---|
| | | | | |
| SOUND | ACTION | REFLECTING | SENSATION | TASTE |
| | | | | |

**\* The sentences in bold should be the students' own, original ideas.**

1.

2.

**3.**

4.

5.

**6.**

7.

8.

**9.**

10.

11.

**12.**

13.

14.

**15.**

## MAKE THREE PARAGRAPHS FROM THE SENTENCES

Paragraph one:

Paragraph two:

Paragraph three:

# MOUNTAINS

## COLOUR

| 1 point | 2 points | 3 points | 4 points | 5 points | TOTAL |
|---------|----------|----------|----------|----------|-------|
| do_e-white | sea__ell-white | flo___-white | an__l-white | h__o-white | |
| bo_e-white | vam__re-white | pha___m-white | li_e-white | f__g-white | |

### MAKE A SENTENCE

1.

2.

## AVALANCHE SOUNDS                    TOTAL

| cra__ing | rum__ing | bo__ing | gr__bling | be__o_ing | |
|----------|----------|---------|-----------|-----------|--|
| cl__ping | ro__ing | tru_dling | gr_w_ing | th_d_ing | |

### MAKE A SENTENCE

1.

2.

## SHAPE                    TOTAL

| crin_led | cru__led | kno__ed | gri__led | ru__ed | |
|----------|----------|---------|----------|--------|--|
| wrin_led | cra__y | ja__ed | gnar__d | ru__e | |

### MAKE A SENTENCE

1.

2.

## ACTION                    TOTAL

| sky-punc_ing | sky-sta__ing | heaven-to__ing | snow-cl__d | snow-wr__d | |
|--------------|--------------|----------------|------------|------------|--|
| sky-pier_ing | sky-spe__ing | heaven-ki__ing | snow-ho__d | snow-fes__d | |

## MAKE A SENTENCE

1.

2

## PATHETIC FALLACY                    TOTAL

| The ank_e | The l__ | The h__ | The s____r | The cr___ | |
|-----------|---------|---------|------------|-----------|---|
| The fo_t | The kn__ | The e___w | The n___ | The fur____d br__ | |

## MAKE A SENTENCE

1.

2.

## SIMILES                    TOTAL

| like arr_w tips | like saw's te__h | like a ro_ of th__ns | like stal_g___es | like a dr__on's b___ | |
|-----------------|------------------|----------------------|------------------|----------------------|---|
| like sha_k's fins | like harp__n tips | like a ro_ of fa__s | like upturn__ stal_c__es | like a ha_'s t__h | |

## MAKE A SENTENCE

1.

2.

## OTHER IMAGES                    TOTAL

| insec_-like fig_res | the gho_t-grey mi_t | a wee__ng waterfall | a l___y s_y | an abo_i__le sn__m_ | |
|---------------------|---------------------|---------------------|-------------|---------------------|---|
| clat__ring deer | a dew-s__ver lake | a nec___ce of snow | a scr___ng ea__e | an iride___t ra__b_w | |

## MAKE A SENTENCE

1.

2.

## SENSATION

| 2 points | 3 points | 5 points | TOTAL |
|----------|----------|----------|-------|
| i_e cold | chi___ng | ar__ic cold | |
| fr____ng | nu___ng | S__er__n cold | |

### MAKE A SENTENCE

1.

2.

## SMELL                        TOTAL

| ste__d mutton | chargr____d lamb | fl__h-fr__d beef | |
|---------------|------------------|------------------|--|
| pot ro__t | a bu____ng broth | a si____ng steak | |

### MAKE A SENTENCE

1.

2.

## TASTE                        TOTAL

| astr_l | co__ic | ast____al | |
|--------|--------|-----------|--|
| ste__ar | gal__ic | othe__r_ly | |

### MAKE A SENTENCE

1.

2.

# PLANNING A PARAGRAPH

The same system of planning should be repeated at least three times. This is to establish its method and importance to the students. It may take some practice, no matter what the level, to reinforce the concept of the 'artist's eye'. It is also a memory exercise if needed and a fun-packed way to add an element of competition to the learning process. If the parent or teacher wishes, more paragraphs may be added. This might include the emotional responses of the student to the scene involved.

| COLOUR | SHAPE | P. FALLACY | IMAGES | SMELL |
|--------|-------|-----------|--------|-------|
|        |       |           |        |       |
| SOUND  | ACTION | SIMILES  | SENSATION | TASTE |
|        |       |           |        |       |

| COLOUR | SHAPE | P.FALLACY | IMAGES | SMELL |
|--------|-------|-----------|--------|-------|
|        |       |           |        |       |
| SOUND  | ACTION | SIMILES  | SENSATION | TASTE |
|        |       |           |        |       |

**\* The sentences in bold should be the students' own, original ideas.**

1.

2.

**3.**

4.

5.

**6.**

7.

8.

**9.**

10.

11.

**12.**

13.

14.

**15.**

### MAKE THREE PARAGRAPHS FROM THE SENTENCES

Paragraph one:

Paragraph two:

Paragraph three:

# THE BEACH

## COLOUR

| 1 point | 2 points | 3 points | 4 points | 5 points | TOTAL |
|---------|----------|----------|----------|----------|-------|
| a but__r-gold beach | a moon gli_t-gold beach | a su__se-gold beach | a li___ni__-gold beach | an ear__li__t-gold beach | |
| a fla_-gold beach | a moon gl_w-gold beach | a su__et-gold beach | a mot__r lo_e-gold beach | an ear__sh__e-gold beach | |

### MAKE A SENTENCE

1.

2.

## SOUND                                                                 TOTAL

| a sle_py sea | a do_y sea | a slot_f_l sea | a slu__e_ing sea | a rep___ng sea | |
|--------------|------------|----------------|------------------|----------------|--|
| a sno_zy sea | a dre__y sea | a slu__i_h sea | a sup__e sea | a lang___o_s sea | |

### MAKE A SENTENCE

1.

2.

## SHAPE                                                                 TOTAL

| an ar_ of beach | a h__k of beach | a sic__e of beach | a do_e of beach | a cr__k of beach | |
|-----------------|-----------------|-------------------|-----------------|------------------|--|
| a bo_ of beach | a hors_s__e of beach | a scy__e of beach | a hal_-m__n of beach | a cre__nt of beach | |

### MAKE A SENTENCE

1.

2.

## METAPHORS WITH THICK LIGHT                 TOTAL

| lant__ns of light | to__rs of light | wa__s of light | st_e__s of light | pi___rs of light | |
|---|---|---|---|---|---|
| cyli__ers of light | sh__ts of light | ri__rs of light | st_e___rs of light | co_u__s of light | |

### MAKE A SENTENCE

1.

2.

## TANS                 TOTAL

| n_t-brown | co__er-brown | sun-bl__t_d | Da_-G_o | pe__a-ta_ | |
|---|---|---|---|---|---|
| leat__r-brown | coc_n__-brown | sun-sta__ed | aft__-gl__ | ube_-ta_ | |

### MAKE A SENTENCE

1.

2.

## KNITTING TERMS FOR A SEA SKY                 TOTAL

| edg_d | kni__ed | s_n | la_d | se__ed | |
|---|---|---|---|---|---|
| thre__ed | stit__ed | fr_ged | he_ed | emb__id__d | |

### MAKE A SENTENCE

1.

2.

## OTHER IMAGES                 TOTAL

| ki_es fl_pping | do__eys br_y_ng | se_g_ls sq_awk_ng | b___s bo__ing | se_ ri___ng | |
|---|---|---|---|---|---|
| c_ild_en scre__ing | ho__es whin__ing | se_g_ls squ__bli_g | yac__s lo_ing | wa__s cre__ng | |

## MAKE A SENTENCE

1.

2.

### SENSATION

| 2 points | 3 points | 5 points | TOTAL |
|---|---|---|---|
| sun ba__d | hea_ <br> gr__led | gl__e <br> ch__red | |
| sun to__ted | hea_ <br> ro___ed | gl__e <br> sc__ch_d | |

## MAKE A SENTENCE

1.

2.

### SMELL     TOTAL

| sa__y | o__y | br__k__h | |
|---|---|---|---|
| chl__ine | ta_gy | sa__ne | |

## MAKE A SENTENCE

1.

2.

### TASTE     TOTAL

| spi_y <br> sau_es | barb_c_ed <br> chic___ | br__y <br> lo__er | |
|---|---|---|---|
| coa_-fired <br> pe__ers | sulf_r__s <br> mu___rd | fr__d <br> _n_o_s | |

## MAKE A SENTENCE

1.

2.

# PLANNING A PARAGRAPH

This template shall remain blank as it may be used later for any of the chapters. Another idea would be to encourage filling in the grids for a chapter not yet covered. For example, the colours, sounds, shape etc. of a lake could be attempted without the student having prior knowledge of it. The educator can call out the titles of the grids and give hints to the possible answers. Prompts are easily given. A typical question might be; what is the quietest place in the world? The answer would then enable the student to fill in the second grid, which is 'The Silent Valley'. In this way, the creative juices are flowing and points may be awarded for the best answers. Whether they match those in the grids or not should be irrelevant as long as the answers are appropriate to the question asked. Making the students think for themselves is one of the core functions of an educator. If they are thinking and you are merely germinating ideas, it is a successful session!

| | | | | |
|---|---|---|---|---|
| | | | | |
| | | | | |
| | | | | |

| | | | | |
|---|---|---|---|---|
| | | | | |
| | | | | |
| | | | | |

**\* The sentences in bold should be the students' own, original ideas.**

1.

2.

**3.**

4.

5.

**6.**

7.

**8.**

**9.**

10.

11.

**12.**

13.

14.

**15.**

## MAKE THREE PARAGRAPHS FROM THE SENTENCES

Paragraph one:

Paragraph two:

Paragraph three:

# WATERFALLS

## COLOUR

| 1 point | 2 points | 3 points | 4 points | 5 points | TOTAL |
|---------|----------|----------|----------|----------|-------|
| ar_tic-blue | Atla___c-blue | Pac___c-blue | Car_b_e__-blue | la___n-blue | |
| aqua__um-blue | Atla___s-blue | Med_te__a_e_n-blue | Ne___ne-blue | rip__i_n-blue | |

### MAKE A SENTENCE

1.

2.

## GENTLE WATERFALL SOUNDS     TOTAL

| dri__ing | gu__ing | spr__ing | sh__e_ing | spr____ing | |
|----------|---------|----------|-----------|------------|--|
| dri__ling | gu___ing | swi__ing | sp___ing | spl____ing | |

### MAKE A SENTENCE

1.

2.

## LOUD WATERFALL SOUNDS     TOTAL

| ru_hing | sur__ng | sm___ing | cla__r_s | wh__s_ing | |
|---------|---------|----------|----------|-----------|--|
| pou__ing | boi__ng | thu__e_ing | clan_o__us | cac_ph__ous | |

### MAKE A SENTENCE

1.

2.

## ACTION     TOTAL

| flo_ed | swo__ed | cra__ed | su__ed | spi__led | |
|--------|---------|---------|--------|----------|--|
| tum__ed | plu__ed | top__ed | plu_e_ed | cas__d_d | |

### MAKE A SENTENCE

1.

2.

## A DIVINITY POOL                                    TOTAL

| inf__ity-pool | ser__ity-pool | ecst__y-pool | rap___e-pool | ete__i__-pool | |
|---|---|---|---|---|---|
| bl_ss-pool | myst__ue-pool | ench_n__e_t-pool | rhap___y-pool | tra__u_l___-pool | |

### MAKE A SENTENCE

1.

2.

## TEXTURE WITH SIMILES                               TOTAL

| like si_k | like su__e | like v___et | like liq__d ho__y | like a loo_ of d_w | |
|---|---|---|---|---|---|
| like sa__n | like sy__p | like vel__r | like al_mi___m | like li___d me__u_y | |

### MAKE A SENTENCE

1.

2.

## OTHER IMAGES                                       TOTAL

| gra__es swa_ing | fr__s cro__ing | ge__e gr__ing | wil___s wil_ing | cas___es sis__ng | |
|---|---|---|---|---|---|
| flo__rs nod_ing | fi__ dar__ng | he__ns spe__ing | wag_a__s bo__ing | cat__a_ts sus_u__t_ng | |

### MAKE A SENTENCE

1.

2.

## SENSATION

2 points    3 points    5 points    TOTAL

| sha_ing | tre__ing | qu__e__ng | |
|---|---|---|---|
| shi__ing | shu___ing | qu__i | |

## MAKE A SENTENCE

1.

2.

### SMELL                   TOTAL

| ho__y sweet | nou__t sweet | gl___se sweet | |
|---|---|---|---|
| trea__e sweet | sy__p sweet | ne___r sweet | |

## MAKE A SENTENCE

1.

2.

### TASTE                   TOTAL

| hea__nly | ang___c | une____ly | |
|---|---|---|---|
| div__e | Go__y | am__o i l | |

## MAKE A SENTENCE

1.

2.

# TEACHING 'ZOOM' NARRATION

'Zoom' narration is when you describe a feature from a distance and gradually change the description as you get closer to it. The grids beneath describe the sights and sounds of a waterfall. As the student gets closer to it, the words they use should change accordingly. Planning it should be made easier with the grids.

## FAR-AWAY SOUNDS

| LEVEL 1 | LEVEL 2 | LEVEL 3 | LEVEL 4 | LEVEL 5 |
|---------|---------|---------|---------|---------|
| hum_ing | murm__ing | thr__ming | rin__ng | ti_ling |
| pur_ing | bur_ling | str__ming | ch__ing | pli__ing |

## FAR-AWAY VIEW

| LEVEL 1 | LEVEL 2 | LEVEL 3 | LEVEL 4 | LEVEL 5 |
|---------|---------|---------|---------|---------|
| a silver slid_ | a blue wav_ | a silver ram_ | a blue wei_ | a silver casc__e |
| a silver shee_ | a blue chut_ | a silver loo_ | a blue funne_ | a silver catar__t |

## CLOSE-UP SOUNDS

| LEVEL 1 | LEVEL 2 | LEVEL 3 | LEVEL 4 | LEVEL 5 |
|---------|---------|---------|---------|---------|
| boi_ing | poun_ing | thund__ous | clam__ous | thres_ing |
| roa_ing | smas_ing | who__hing | clan_rous | cac__honous |

## CLOSE-UP VIEW

| LEVEL 1 | LEVEL 2 | LEVEL 3 | LEVEL 4 | LEVEL 5 |
|---------|---------|---------|---------|---------|
| bub_les of spray | mi_t-like spray | tran_e-like spray | eter__ty-pool | like quic__il_er |
| air_ spray | drea_y spray | mir_ge-like | infin__y-pool | like a water wit__es' robe |

## FLOWING 'S' SOUNDS

| LEVEL 1 | LEVEL 2 | LEVEL 3 | LEVEL 4 | LEVEL 5 |
|---------|---------|---------|---------|---------|
| spil_ed | smo_t_ly | like liq__d | sens__us | sve__e |

| | | sil_er | | |
|---|---|---|---|---|
| sl_d | sli_ped | sle_k | su_ple | sy__h-like |

More grids can be added to this. It would be a good idea to discuss any other activity around the waterfall. It could be the fish in a pool, the vegetation in the water or the types of birds and animals you might encounter. Whatever gets the student thinking is worth the effort!

# THE FOREST

## COLOUR

| 1 point | 2 points | 3 points | 4 points | 5 points | TOTAL |
|---|---|---|---|---|---|
| bam__o-brown | te_k-brown | con__r-brown | um__r-brown | ma___a_y-brown | |
| n_t-brown | tan_in-brown | o__-brown | be__h-brown | a_m__d-brown | |

### MAKE A SENTENCE

1.

2.

## SOUND                              TOTAL

| cre__ing trees | cri__ly flo_r | cla__ing bo__hs | cra___ing le___s | ru__ling fo__a_e | |
|---|---|---|---|---|---|
| cr__c_ing twigs | cr__py gr___es | cra__ly fe__s | sn___ng br____es | ph__- ph___ing nuts | |

### MAKE A SENTENCE

1.

2.

## METAPHORS                              TOTAL

| cas__es | hi_h ri_es | for_r____s | car_t___rs | sle___g so__s | |
|---|---|---|---|---|---|
| tow__s | sk__cr__ers | cita___s | gua__i__s | pul___g he___s | |

### MAKE A SENTENCE

1.

2.

## ANIMAL SOUNDS

TOTAL

| snuf_ling boa_ | scam__ring hares | scree__ing jays | sham___ng ba__ers | lo___g wo___s | |
|---|---|---|---|---|---|
| slin_ing wil_ca_s | scur__ing squ__rels | scu__ling ra___ts | ski____ing mice | lum____g be__s | |

## MAKE A SENTENCE

1.

2.

## THE SHAPE OF STARS

TOTAL

| lumi_o_s pet__s | luc_d snowf___es | lamb__t aste_s | lum__o_s pr__ks | luc__t pen__gr__s | |
|---|---|---|---|---|---|
| of silver | of silver | of shin_ silver | of gli__ing silver | of fla__ing silver | |

## MAKE A SENTENCE

1.

2.

## EDIBLES OF THE FOREST

TOTAL

| mus_r__ms | be___es | wil_bas_l | stin_ing ne__e | plant__n | |
|---|---|---|---|---|---|
| n__s | woo_ sor__l | wil_ ga_i_ | chi__we_d | fai__rin_ champ__n_n | |

## MAKE A SENTENCE

1.

2.

## OTHER IMAGES

TOTAL

| moss-vei__d trail | sha_y gla_s | clu__s of mos_ | ho__y bou_s | lea_y can__y | |
|---|---|---|---|---|---|
| lea_-carp__ed path | reac__ng tre_s | sec__t gro_s | dru__ing woo_pe__ers | Ju_a_i_ fe__s | |

## MAKE A SENTENCE

1.

2.

## SENSATION

| 2 points | 3 points | 5 points | TOTAL |
|---|---|---|---|
| heart-<br>war__ng | soul-<br>so___ing | soul_swe___ng | |
| heart-<br>comfo__ing | soul-<br>no__i__ing | soul-ha_____g | |

## MAKE A SENTENCE

1.

2.

## SMELL     TOTAL

| | | | |
|---|---|---|---|
| eart_y | org___c | mu__y | |
| pul_y | seas__d | lo__y | |

## MAKE A SENTENCE

1.

2.

## TASTE     TOTAL

| | | | |
|---|---|---|---|
| fru__y | me___w<br>sweet | tr___e<br>sweet | |
| orch__d<br>sweet | sh___y<br>sweet | m__d<br>sweet | |

## MAKE A SENTENCE

1.

2.

# TEACHING A DIARY ENTRY

The diary is your dog. This is a controversial statement, but it is true. A dog is your best friend. You can tell him your innermost secrets, your darkest fears and your most precious hopes for the future. Unlike some humans, he will never betray you by telling someone else. That is why you should tell your diary everything. Treat the diary the same as a conversation that you would have with a dog about the day just gone. Use the K.I.S.S philosophy also- Keep It Simple, Silly! There is no need to use big, awkward words as you probably wouldn't put them in your own diary. Underneath is a list of 'Do's' and 'Don't's'.

| | |
|---|---|
| Do use the past tense mostly. It's a mini-memoir of the day just gone. | Don't use the present tense unless you are at your desk writing a diary entry. |
| Do use short sentences. You are writing to yourself. | Don't complicate the syntax, the sentence construction, with long sentences. |
| Do explore as many emotions as the day just gone requires. | Don't just rattle off emotions in a list. Explain why you felt as you did. |
| Do use train-of-thought. This means write it as you felt it. | Don't ramble or use too much formal language. Keep it simple, silly. |
| Do use the diary as a self-exorcism of sorts. Use the diary to get things off your chest. | Don't use excessively emotional language unless the situation warranted it. |
| Do mention features of nature that you encountered, but don't over-indulge. | Don't use too much omniscient (descriptive) language. A diary doesn't want to know. |
| Do use humour as a writing technique that everyone can enjoy. | Don't put in too many big words (grandiloquent language). |
| Do use rhetorical questions that can only be answered by you. It varies the writing style. | Don't over punctuate, put in quotation marks or direct speech. It is not a novel. |
| Do use the future tense at the end of the diary entry. Look forward with joy or dread to tomorrow. | Don't use the past continuous tense where possible (i.e. I **was walking**). **I walked** is fine. It will trip you up if you try it. |
| Do remember to 'sign in' with Dear diary and 'sign off' however you please. | Don't forget to sign off! **'Bye for now** or **'Till tomorrow** is fine. |

There really is no such thing as different levels of language in a diary entry. There are merely different patterns of thought and structure. By employing techniques such as humour and rhetorical questions, a student can have a very engaging and enjoyable diary. If a student is asked to write the diary of James Joyce, there is an argument to be made for flowery, ornate language. Otherwise, it should be more like Forrest Gump; short on verbosity, but packed with emotion! The next page includes a sample diary entry of a student going on a school trip to a forest; a real one, not a Gump! The emotions are in bold and the rest of the diary should be finished by the students in simple language. The educator should also make out a grid of emotions based on the student's level of ability. The categories could be: happy emotions, sad emotions, overjoyed emotions, angry emotions and self-confident emotions etc.

# DIARY ENTRY FOR A FOREST OUTING

Dear diary;

Why oh why does the world **hate** me so? My English teacher told us yesterday not to use big words when writing a diary but what does he know about catastrophe? Has he seen the end of the world like I have seen it, the end of days? Stupid forest. Stupid bees and stupid teachers. Look at my face. I feel **horrified**.

The shame of it is that I was **enjoying** myself. We pulled up on the bus and I have to admit it was beautiful. It was a leafy paradise with ferns like something out of a Tolkein novel. The birds were carolling, the bees (those damned bees!) were humming like hairdryers and everyone was excited. Even my stony heart was **happy** for a short time. I knew it couldn't last though. Billy No-Mates was given special permission by the principal to come on this trip. Even his mother doesn't leave him outside. How in the name of god did the principal think it would work out? You know how he is, diary. I might have mentioned him before. Serial killer eyes, his knuckles scrape the ground when he walks and he has a mad cackle instead of a laugh. He **disgusts** me because he's a bully.

What he did to us with that bees nest was **shameful**…..

# LAKES

## COLOUR

| 1 point | 2 points | 3 points | 4 points | 5 points | TOTAL |
|---|---|---|---|---|---|
| mir__r-silver | diamo__-fla_e silver | sta_ fi__-silver | orr_s-silver | verg__s-silver | |
| skyli_e-silver | dew glea_-silver | tea___op-silver | arge_t-silver | fra__l-silver | |

## MAKE A SENTENCE

1.

2.

## THE SILENT VALLEY                    TOTAL

| ca_e quiet | conv__t quiet | nun___y quiet | cloi___r quiet | wo__ quiet | |
|---|---|---|---|---|---|
| cav__n quiet | cath___al quiet | mona____y quiet | confes____al quiet | to__ quiet | |

## MAKE A SENTENCE

1.

2.

## THE CLEAR LAKE                    TOTAL

| win__w clear | g_n clear | dia___d clear | var___h clear | lacq__r clear | |
|---|---|---|---|---|---|
| pan_ clear | vo__a clear | deca___r clear | ven__r clear | moo_s__n_ clear | |

## MAKE A SENTENCE

1.

2.

## THE STILL LAKE                                    TOTAL

| sta__e still | yog_ still | va__t still | fen_ shu_ still | ossu__y still | |
|---|---|---|---|---|---|
| shri_e still | Bud_h_ still | cry_t still | Ze_ still | sarco___g s still | |

## MAKE A SENTENCE

1.

2.

## FISH SOUNDS                                    TOTAL

| buc__ng | thu__ing | flo__ing | plo___g | plu___g | |
|---|---|---|---|---|---|
| di_e-bom__ng | plu___ng | fl__-flo__ing | pli_-plo___g | ke_-plu___g | |

## MAKE A SENTENCE

1.

2.

## THE FLY ARMY                                    TOTAL

| an ar__ | a leg__n | a squ___on | a pla__n | a bri__e | |
|---|---|---|---|---|---|
| a mo_ | a divi___n | a reg___nt | a pha___x | a bat___on | |

## MAKE A SENTENCE

1.

2.

## A MOMENT OF CLARITY                                    TOTAL

| an 'ah_' moment | a lig_t b__b moment | an eur__a moment | an hosa__a moment | an all_l__a moment | |
|---|---|---|---|---|---|
| a 'za_' moment | a li__tn__g moment | an epi___ny | a rev__t_t__n | a hal_e_u_ah | |

1.

2.

## SENSATIONS OF PAIN

| 2 points | 3 points | 5 points | TOTAL |
|---|---|---|---|
| bi_ing fli_s | st___ing be__ | ni___ng mi__es | |
| itc_ing gra__ | pr___ing thi__les | pi___ing a__s | |

## MAKE A SENTENCE

1.

2.

| **SMELL** | | | TOTAL |
|---|---|---|---|
| s_p sweet | nirv__a sweet | sac_h___ne sweet | |
| Ed__ sweet | utop__ sweet | Z__n sweet | |

## MAKE A SENTENCE

1.

2.

| **TASTE** | | | TOTAL |
|---|---|---|---|
| cri_p water | spr__g fre__ | crys_a__ine taste | |
| gla__y water | taste of spr__e | tun__a pur_ | |

## MAKE A SENTENCE

1.

2.

# HELPING STUDENTS TO THINK

Everyone sees, but very few observe. That is probably true of most students, especially those living in an urban environment. One cannot blame the modern student for leaning towards the survival skills necessary in the modern world. Imparting an appreciation of nature is a gift to them, however. Nature goes hand-in-hand with self-reflection, an awareness of self and a sense of where we are placed in the grand theatre of life. Some simple exercises can help to foster a healthy regard for the complexity and scope of nature. Take the student/class outside and ask them to write down what they see around them. When they have finished, question if they have included: the clouds or sky, the birds or insects, the trees or grass and the sounds or texture of the natural world. Higher order thinkers see the world in a different way. It may be divided into five basic categories. These are:

1. Colour- clouds, sky, trees, grass, moon etc.

2. Sound- soft, loud, distant, near, high pitched etc.

3. Shape- the contours and outlines of all aspects of nature.

4. Action (or inaction) - of all aspects of nature.

5. Texture- of grass, water, a beach etc. Is it rough, smooth, liquid, soft, hard, fluffy or gritty?

There are some simple ways to teach students to think like this. It merely takes practise, patience and praise. Pick the clouds, for example. Are they dove-white or gravel-grey? Is it possible to say they are whispering across the sky or are they simply brooding in silence? Are they puffy like pillows or are they boiling like tar? Are they ghosting or racing across the sky? Do they seem soft like cotton or liquid-filled like pitch?

It is possible to apply three or four of the basic categories to all features of nature. Grids should be made out in the vocabulary notebook with these five headings. Even if a guest speaker has to come in or an outing organised, compiling a list of birds, their colour and their movements in the air should be encouraged. A similar list for types of native animals and the edibles with their seasons should also be included.

Finally, the three senses of sensation, smell and taste should be referred to also. If the grass feels as cool as silk, the scent of pine is in the air and even the air itself tastes fresh and crisp, the educator is doing a wonderful job. Using creative metaphors, similes and lucid imagery will add to the menu of excellence. The last technique to master is laser-eyed attention to detail. Underneath is a grid that may help the students. The educator should use the grid as a fill in the blanks exercise, giving prompts only where necessary.

| | clouds | birds | sky | insects | trees | grass |
|---|---|---|---|---|---|---|
| colour | halo-white | iridescent plumage | Jerusalem-blue | bat-black cave-black | bark-brown nut-brown | Eden-green aphid-green |
| sound | womb silent | carolling lilting | silent voiceless | chittering droning | rustling | whispering |
| shape/action | tufty/ gliding | sickle wings | dome/hanging | skittering scuttling | mushroom domed | mini-fronds waving |
| texture | cotton | downy | like velvet | gritty | crusty | satin |
| surrounding smells | funfair of smells | earthy loamy mulchy | peach sweet pollen sweet petal sweet | pine mint thyme | resin woody incense | sap sweet chlorophyll pulpy |
| sensations | blissful | soul warming | spirit lifting | heart stopping | awe inspiring | energizing |

Repeat this exercise with the flora and fauna of a river scene, a beach scene etc. The educator is giving the student a priceless gift; a multisensory awareness of his/her surroundings. Eventually, after practice, the student will be able to replace **description** with **visualisation**. Then, hopefully, the student will no longer be confined by the limits of his/her imagination.

# SPRING

## COLOUR

| 1 point | 2 points | 3 points | 4 points | 5 points | TOTAL |
|---|---|---|---|---|---|
| pe_-green | gla_e-green | mi__-green | fai__la_d-green | pa__d__e-green | |
| pars__y-green | gra_e-green | mala___te-green | fai__ta_e-green | won___la_d-green | |

## MAKE A SENTENCE

1.

2.

## SOUND                     TOTAL

| blea_ing lam_s | chi__ing ch_cks | yip___g fox cu_s | spl___er_ng law_m___rs | pal_t__ing heart of spring | |
|---|---|---|---|---|---|
| low__g ca_ves | cro___ng pige_ns | whin__ing fo_ls | sn__ing sh_ars | thr_b__g heart of nat__e | |

## MAKE A SENTENCE

1.

2.

## SIMILES FOR THE MOON              TOTAL

| like a shim__ring dis_ | like a glea_ing glo_e | like a glo__ng or_ | like a shi__ salv__ | like a fres__y_-mi__ed coi_ | |
|---|---|---|---|---|---|
| of silver | of gold | of gold | of silver | | |

## MAKE A SENTENCE

1.

2.

## THE MOVEMENT OF SCENTS          TOTAL

| bl_w | dri_d | gl_ed | pu_ed | sw__ed | |
|------|-------|-------|-------|--------|--|
| car__ed | flo__ed | ho__ed | perc__a_d | dra__ed | |

## MAKE A SENTENCE

1.

2.

## SPRING FLOWERS          TOTAL

| dais__s | dand__i_ns | peo__s | prim_o_s | da_o__s | |
|---------|-----------|--------|----------|---------|--|
| but__rc_ps | tu_i_s | cro_u_es | ho__ys_k_e | b_e_e__s | |

## MAKE A SENTENCE

1.

2.

## METAPHORS FOR THIN LIGHT          TOTAL

| strin_s | staf_s | ar__s | ri_o_s | la_rs | |
|---------|--------|-------|--------|-------|--|
| stran_s | shaf_s | sp_rs | fi_g_s | la_es | |

## MAKE A SENTENCE

1.

2.

## OTHER IMAGES          TOTAL

| spla_-legged lam_s | ope_-bea_ed chi_s | mis_y-e_ed fo_ c_s | tur__e-slo_ la__m_w__s | tu__o-win__d bla_b__s | |
|--------------------|-------------------|--------------------|------------------------|-----------------------|--|
| mil_-splas__d ca_ves | prou_-brea_ed pig_o_s | sta_-bla_d fo_s | sca__l-sh_p she_s | yo_k-y_lo_ du__li_gs | |

## MAKE A SENTENCE

1.

2.

### SENSATION

| 2 points | 3 points | 5 points | TOTAL |
|---|---|---|---|
| co_l | soot__ng | car_s_i_g | |
| plea__t | sal_i_g | ru_f__ng | |

### MAKE A SENTENCE

1.

2.

### SMELL TOTAL

| | | | TOTAL |
|---|---|---|---|
| ba__d<br>ap__e | cand__d | conf__t__n__y | |
| cr__m<br>sw__t | cara__l | tu__i-fr__i | |

### MAKE A SENTENCE

1.

2.

### TASTE TOTAL

| | | | TOTAL |
|---|---|---|---|
| flo_al | pe__l<br>sweet | mola__es<br>sweet | |
| can_y fl__s<br>sweet | blo___m<br>sweet | meri__e<br>sweet | |

### MAKE A SENTENCE

1.

2.

# SPRING GREENS AND BLUES

The grid below is designed to help the student use a splash of colour in their writing. The colours should scorch across the page, enthralling the reader. Because this is a workbook, one or two letters are missing from each. The good news is that the solutions are at the back of the book! Each word has been carefully designed to be easily accessible with a dictionary, a thesaurus or a computer. The educator should find that each student will have their favourites, colours which resonate with them and them alone. That is because the texture of the colour they like grabs their attention. By using these colours, their passage or essay will be transformed. Hopefully, even the educator will learn something from the grid also. Anyone who attempts to fill them in can add up their tally of colours at the end of the grids. If you get over twenty seven without the dictionary, you are a certified genius! The next chapter shall explain how many colours should be used in a passage of writing.

| 30 basic blues | 30 advanced blues | 30 basic greens | 30 advanced greens |
|---|---|---|---|
| alpi_e-blue | aquam_r_ne-blue | Ama_on-green | aph_d-green |
| a_uari_m-blue | Arcad_an-blue | carni_al-green | b_ize-green |
| ast_al-blue | Atlant_s-blue | cele_y-green | ber_l-green |
| bilbe_ry-blue | aur_ra Austra_is | Ed_n-green | carou_el-green |
| bro_hure-blue | auro_a bore_lis | fe_n-green | chartreu_e-green |
| bu__erf_y-blue | Baby_on-blue | fore_t-green | chlor_ph_ll-green |
| che_ic_l-blue | bli_s-blue | garni_h-green | cy_n-green |
| co_k_ail-blue | celes_ial-blue | gra_e-green | encha_t_ent-green |
| cos_ic-blue | cerul_an-blue | gl_de-green | fair_la_d-green |
| cr_s_al-blue | constel_ati_n-blue | ja_e-green | fair_ta_e-green |
| dra_o_f_y-blue | divi_e-blue | jui_y-green | fores_er-green |
| du_k-e_g blue | Empyre_n-blue | l_ke-green | garla_d-green |
| ele_tr_c-blue | fanta_y-blue | marb_e-green | jasp_r-green |
| ga_fl_me-blue | firmam_nt-blue | mea_ow-green | Jer_sal_m-green |
| ge_st_ne-blue | gala_y-blue | mil_y-green | lapi_ laz_li-green |
| gla_ier-blue | halog_n-blue | m_nt-green | luscio_s-green |
| ice_int-blue | nirv_na-blue | m_ss-green | malachi_e-green |

| | | | |
|---|---|---|---|
| Jes_s-blue | nitro_s-blue | p_a-green | mis_ val_ey-green |
| jew_l-blue | peac_ck-blue | pep_er_int-green | parad_se-green |
| kin_fis_er-blue | pellu_id-blue | pinemi_t-green | pristi_e-green |
| lag_on-blue | Prus_ian-blue | post_ard-green | sacr_d-green |
| lumi_o_s-blue | rapt_re-blue | r_ed-green | stor_b_ok-green |
| n_on-blue | ripar_an-blue | s_ge-green | tourmal_ne-green |
| plas_a-blue | sere_e-blue | s_p-green | utopi_n-green |
| pow_er-blue | Sibe_ian-blue | s_a-green | verda_t-green |
| sa_ph_re-blue | strato_pher_c-blue | sizz_i_g-green | verb_na-green |
| sol_r-blue | top_z-blue | sprin_ le_f-green | vires_ent-green |
| te_l-blue | ultr_ma_ine-blue | velv_t-green | will_w-green |
| uni_er_e-blue | wanderl_st-blue | water_ress-green | wond_rl__d-green |
| wo_d-blue | Ze_s-blue | woo_pine-green | Zi_n-green |
| TOTAL= | TOTAL= | TOTAL= | TOTAL= |

# SUMMER

## COLOUR

| 1 point | 2 points | 3 points | 4 points | 5 points | TOTAL |
|---|---|---|---|---|---|
| plu_-purple sk__s | juni__r-purple suns__s | amet__st-purple sk__s | orpi__-purple sk__s | mona___y-purple sun_i__s | |
| heat__r-purple sk__s | mulb___y-purple suns__s | mage__a-purple sk__s | Tyr__n-purple sk__s | roy__-purple glo__ing | |

## MAKE A SENTENCE

1.

2.

## BEE MUSIC                                        TOTAL

| bu__ing bees | dro__ng bees | mum___ng bees | the murm___t__n of bees | the c_lt-h__ of bees | |
|---|---|---|---|---|---|
| hu__ing bees | into__ng bees | mur___ing of bees | the mus_it___on of bees | the mo__-h__ of bees | |

## MAKE A SENTENCE

1.

2.

## METAPHORS FOR THE SUN                           TOTAL

| a dazz___ng circle | a fla__ing fi__ba__ | a gli__e_ing e_e | a fl___g wh__l | a fi__y r__g | |
|---|---|---|---|---|---|
| of chr_me-gold | of ma__a-red | of lum___us-gold | of saf___n-orange | of l__a-red | |

## MAKE A SENTENCE

1.

38

2.

## THE DAWN CHORUS                                            TOTAL

| a bea_ed conc__t | a feat__r_d mel__y | an av__n ari_ | a caro___ng op__a | a win__d s_mp___y | |
|---|---|---|---|---|---|
| a bea_ed cho_us | a fea__er_d medl_y | an anci__t alch__y of song | a quav__ing orc___t_a | a win__d sorc__y | |

## MAKE A SENTENCE

1.

2.

## EDIBLE FOODS                                               TOTAL

| wil_ th_me | rams__s | bilb___y | chant__e__e | gia__ puf_b__l | |
|---|---|---|---|---|---|
| ce_ | shag_y in_c_p | blac_ mus__r_ | sw__t vio_t | par_s_l mus_r__m | |

## MAKE A SENTENCE

1.

2.

## THE SWEEP OF SKY                                           TOTAL

| endl__s | ete_n_l | eve_l_t_g | meas_el_s | limi__s | |
|---|---|---|---|---|---|
| unen_i_g | inf_n_t | perp__u_l | imme_sur__e | bou_le_s | |

## MAKE A SENTENCE

1.

2.

## THE BRIGHTEST BLUES                                        TOTAL

| chemi_al-blue | sol__-blue | ele_r__-blue | pola__s-blue | cele_t__l-blue | |
|---|---|---|---|---|---|
| cock__il-blue | broc_re-blue | n__n-blue | pla__a-blue | const___a_i__-blue | |

## MAKE A SENTENCE

1.

2.

### SENSATION

| 2 points | 3 points | 5 points | TOTAL |
|----------|----------|----------|-------|
| feat__r soft | cot__n soft | si__ soft | |
| dow_y soft | ei__r soft | ve__e_ soft | |

## MAKE A SENTENCE

1.

2.

### SMELL

| SMELL | | | TOTAL |
|-------|---|---|-------|
| a so_p of smells | a br__h of smells | a go__a_h of smells | |
| a st_w of smells | a b__w of smells | a bu__et of smells | |

## MAKE A SENTENCE

1.

2.

### TASTE

| TASTE | | | TOTAL |
|-------|---|---|-------|
| loze_ge sweet | hon__s_c__e sweet | mar_i__n sweet | |
| gela_in sweet | cit__s sweet | ma__a sweet | |

## MAKE A SENTENCE

1.

2.

# SUMMER BROWNS AND YELLOWS

Unfortunately, browns and yellows are not as exciting as blues and greens. They are no less effective in an essay, however. There are only thirty colours in each grid as there isn't as wide a spectrum of colour for these summery hues. The question of how many colours to use is an interesting one. I certainly would not encourage any student to use more than two colours per paragraph. Each should be different, lending a carnival of colour for the reader to experience. A good ploy for an educator to use is to ask the student to write down a list of browns before attempting this grid. A point can be awarded for any adjective they can match to the grid below. If they can score more than eight points, they are exceptional. He/she will then see the value of the colours in a different light. In some places, hints are given, as more than one letter could be used to form a different word. In others, it may be a rare word. The educator will then have to look it up in the computer dictionary if the student does not have one.

| 30 summer browns | | 30 summer yellows | |
|---|---|---|---|
| almo_d-brown | | but_er_up-yellow | |
| autu_n-brown | | ca_ary-yellow | |
| bamb_o-brown | | cit_us-yellow | |
| b_rk-brown | | c_rn-yellow | |
| be_r-brown | animal | da__odil-yellow | |
| bisc_it-brown | | gambo_e-yellow | gum resin |
| b_g-brown | wet place | gold se_m-yellow | |
| cara_el-brown | | gold ve_n-yellow | |
| ches_n_t-brown | | hon_ycomb-yellow | |
| cinn_m_n-brown | | lem_n-yellow | |
| coco_ut-brown | | lightn_ng-yellow | |
| conk_r-brown | slang | mari_old-yellow | |
| cop_er-brown | | mel_n-yellow | |
| des_rt-brown | | moon be_m-yellow | |
| _awn-brown | animal | moon fl_me-yellow | |
| k_lp-brown | | moon gl_w-yellow | |

| | | | |
|---|---|---|---|
| maho_any-brown | | mus_ard-yellow | |
| mi_k-brown | animal | orpim_nt-yellow | |
| m_nk-brown | | prim_ose-yellow | |
| mou_y-brown | | saff_on-yellow | |
| n_t-brown | food | sun fla_h-yellow | |
| ott_r-brown | | sunr_se-yellow | |
| ru_set-brown | | sun_et-yellow | |
| ru_t-brown | of metal | syr_p-yellow | |
| st_w-brown | | treac_e-yellow | |
| tan_in-brown | | xant_in-yellow | |
| te_k-brown | tree | y_m-yellow | |
| toa_t-brown | | yea_t-yellow | |
| waf_r-brown | | y_lk-yellow | |
| wa_nut-brown | | zestf_l-yellow | |

# AUTUMN

## COLOUR

| 1 Point | 2 Points | 3 Points | 4 Points | 5 Points | TOTAL |
|---|---|---|---|---|---|
| la_a-red | ma__a-red | bo__i_e-red | inf___o-red | py__-red | |
| emb_r-red | mol__n-red | bar__c_e-red | inc_e__t_r-red | conf_gr__i_n-red | |

1.

2.

## UNUSUAL WIND SOUNDS  TOTAL

| nuzz_ing | ruf___ing | kne___ing | sou___ng | whe___ng | |
|---|---|---|---|---|---|
| huf_ing | yaw__ng | muf___ng | susp___ng | whi___ng | |

1.

2.

## METAPHORS FOR THE CLOUDS  TOTAL

| air_ anvi_s | cosm_c clo_ks | smo_y shi_l_s | hea_e_ly ho__s | ste__y sh_ou_s | |
|---|---|---|---|---|---|
| puf_y plat_s | fluf_y flee_es | bil_o_y be_ls | pu__ing pa_ls | vapo___s ve__s | |

1.

2.

## ARCHAIC WORDS FOR AUTUMN  TOTAL

| leaves a-fi_e | trees a-fla_h | oa_ leaves a-li__t | lea_y do_e a-g__e | ca__py a-sc__ch | |
|---|---|---|---|---|---|
| lea_es a-fla_e | trees a-fli__er | as_ trees a-bl__e | lea_y arc_ a-gl__m | sess__e ca__py a-smo__er | |

1.

2.

## AN AUTUMN FEAST  TOTAL

| slur_ing on bla_kbe_ries | dro__ling over str__be_ries | slo__ering on elde_be_ries | mun____g on wi_d a__les | cr____ing on ha__n__s | |
|---|---|---|---|---|---|
| chom_ing on bla_kbe_ries | gul___g on go_sebe_ries | dri__ling over slo_ber_ies | go__ing on sw__t ch__tn_t | mast__a__ng on wa___ts | |

1.

2.

## COLOURS USING HEAT  TOTAL

| ho_-r_ds | bur__ng br__ns | glo___g-go__s | fev___sh-ye___s | bro____g-o____s | |
|---|---|---|---|---|---|
| fie_y-r_ds | bl__ing br__ns | smou____ing-golds | sco____g-ye___s | swell____g-o____s | |

1.

2.

## OTHER IMAGES FOR AUTUMN  TOTAL

| gh_st-gr_y ski_s | ow_s h__t | the rain dre__hes | gho___y cor_s of mo__li_t | list___s liga___ts of li__t | |
|---|---|---|---|---|---|
| gho_l-gr_y ski_s | ow_s hau_t | the rain dou__s | ee__e ten_r__s of mo_nli_t | the stra____g li__t of au___n | |

1.

2.

## SENSATION

| 2 points | 3 points | 5 points | TOTAL |
|---|---|---|---|
| nervo_s | spoo__d | unh__ged | |
| afr__d | dau__ed | unma___d | |

1.

2.

## SMELL                                                                TOTAL

| a me_u of sme_ls | a perf_me_y of fra_ra__es | a sc_l__ry of fra_ra__es | |
|---|---|---|---|
| a larde_ of sce_ts | a po_-po__ri of ar_m_s | a smorg__b__d of ar_m_s | |

1.

2.

## TASTE                                                                TOTAL

| a savou_y taste | a ravis___g taste | a who___ome taste | |
|---|---|---|---|
| a mou_h-wate__ng taste | an exqu___te taste | a too__s__e tr__t | |

1.

2.

# AUTUMN REDS AND GOLDS

The most vivid colour in the human mind is probably the colour red. It can be a tragic, van Gogh-red or it can be a bright, carnival-red. Personally, I always love the autumn when I get my students to hunt for three different leaves. They are to vary from a mellow red to a warm red to a fiery red. They stick them in their vocabulary notebook with glue. We then put a list of five adjectives underneath each leaf which encapsulates each colour. Its fun, it's different and it's textural. It also acts as a mnemonic device as they find the colours less abstract when they can associate them with an object. The same may be tried for all the colours, even if fabrics or paint have to be used. In a very short time, the class will have the nicest vocabulary notebook to be seen in any school!

| 30  basic reds | 30 advanced reds | 30 glittering golds |
|---|---|---|
| ber_y-red | balef_re-red | Arc-of-_ove_ant gold |
| blo_d-red | braz_er-red | aur_olin-gold |
| bonf_re-red | brimst_ne-red | bee_w_x-gold |
| clar_t-red | clar_t-red | chr_me-gold |
| crim_on-red | conflagr_t_on-red | fla_en-gold |
| dev_l-red | crema_o_ium-red | fulv_us-gold |
| dev_l fl_me-red | crucifi_ion-red | gamb_ge-gold |
| dev_l bl__d-red | dama_k-red | harp st_i_g-gold |
| drag_n bl__d-red | firebr_nd-red | hon_y_omb-gold |
| drag_n fl_me-red | fired_ake-red | hon_y_ew-gold |
| em_er-red | firef_y-red | ing_t-gold |
| fire_all-red | flor_d-red | ligh_n_ng-gold |
| firec_al-red | glow-w_rm-red | lust_ous-gold |
| fire c_re-red | haemogl_bin-red | mar_le-leaf-gold |
| fire fl_me-red | hen_a-red | molt_n-gold |
| fire s_ark-red | incend_ary-red | moon gl_w-gold |
| hel_hou_d-red | marro_ bl_od-red | moon shi_mer-gold |
| hol_y-red | o_blood-red | nec_ar-gold |
| infer_o-red | phoe_ix-red | Nor_ic-gold |

| | | |
|---|---|---|
| la_a-red | rhe_my-red | ore-gold |
| mag_a-red | ro_ge-red | star b_am-gold |
| mercu_y-red | rubic_nd-red | star fl_sh-gold |
| molt_n-red | rushli_ht-red | star str_ak-gold |
| r_se-red | sangui_e-red | suns_t-gold |
| ru_y-red | solf_ri_o-red | sy_up-gold |
| rus_et-red | sor_el-red | trea_le-gold |
| squ_d-red | stam_el-red | Teut_n_c-gold |
| vamp_re's eye-red | Tit_an-red | valk_y_ie-gold |
| windf_ll-red | vermi_ion-red | waxm_lt-gold |
| w_ne-red | vinac_ous-red | as gold as Zeus' thunderbolts |
| TOTAL= | TOTAL= | TOTAL= |

# WINTER

## COLOUR

| 1 Point | 2 Points | 3 Points | 4 Points | 5 Points | TOTAL |
|---|---|---|---|---|---|
| ble_ch-white | ar_ti-white | va___re-white | qui__l_me-white | whe_-white | |
| wha_eb_ne-white | po__r-white | zom__e-white | sk__l-white | cry_t___ine-white | |

1.

2.

## SOUND                                                                 TOTAL

| blas_ing stor_s | flo__ing squa__s | las___g ra_s___s | man___ng w__ds | sund___g cy__o_es | |
|---|---|---|---|---|---|
| batte__ng gus_s | fla__ng th__d__s__rms | lace_at__g hu__i__n_s | ra_ing win__t__ms | evis_e_a_ing tem__s_s | |

1.

2.

## STORMS USING PATHETIC FALLACY                    TOTAL

| scre__ing winds | shri__ing winds | wai__g winds | yow___g winds | kee___g winds | |
|---|---|---|---|---|---|
| scre_ching winds | sna__ing winds | whi__g winds | mew___g winds | cate_w____ng winds | |

1.

2.

## SILENCE                                                              TOTAL

| a qui_t pea_e | a dea_h-lile si__n_e | an awf__ sh__h | an al__n sere_i_y | an une_r___y soun_l__sn__s | |
|---|---|---|---|---|---|
| a gen_le hu_h | a to_b-like sti__n_ss | a ter_i_e ca_m_ess | an ee__e tra_ui_i_y | a shoc___g qui_s___ce | |

1.

2.

## SKY COLOUR
TOTAL

| gri_-grey | fli_t-grey | le__d-grey | shac__e-grey | fet__r-grey | |
|---|---|---|---|---|---|
| gra_el-grey | cind_r-grey | sh__e-grey | man__le-grey | fe_-grey | |

1.

2.

## BARREN SKIES
TOTAL

| emp_y skies | ble_k skies | hau__ing skies | wa_ skies | ske_e_a_ skies | |
|---|---|---|---|---|---|
| lon_ly skies | bit__r skies | pas_y skies | blan__ed skies | cad__er__s skies | |

1.

2.

## CHOKING SKIES
TOTAL

| winter cho_es | winter smo__ers | winter sti__s | winter cons_r__ts | winter gar_o__es | |
|---|---|---|---|---|---|
| winter sq_e_zes | winter str__les | winter suf_o__t_s | winter thr_t__es | winter asphy_ia__s | |

1.

2.

## SMELL
TOTAL

| spi_y beef | mul__d win_ | oak_n ove_ smells | sulph__o_s cra__ers | franki_c__e scen__d ca__les | |
|---|---|---|---|---|---|
| pep_ery sce_ts | mal_ liq_ers | exo__c ove_ sme__s | the wh__f of cord__e from cra__rs | my__h-sce__d ca____s | |

1.

2.

## SENSATION                                                                TOTAL

| shi__ring bod__s | sti_f lim_s | cha__ering te__h | ski_-see__ng co__ | chil_l__ned f__t | |
|---|---|---|---|---|---|
| qui_er_ng bod__s | so_e joi__s | ti__ing fi__er__ps | bra__y-n__es snu__le | hyp_t___m_a and gan_r__e | |

1.

2.

## TASTE                                                                      TOTAL

| sea_oned veget__les | te_tan__ns | spar___ng cha_pa__e | ga_y g__se | fa_-dri__ing du__ | |
|---|---|---|---|---|---|
| bu__ery pot_t_es | mus__oo_ vo_-au-ve_ts | yea__y b__r | pl___y pu____gs | thy__-fi__ed tu____s | |

1.

2.

# WINTER WHITES AND GREYS

The moonstone-white snowscape of winter is a great opportunity to explore the sensations of cold in the human body. Slate-grey clouds with a plum-purple tint herald the first, feathery falls of snow and the nights draw in like a slowly-tightening noose. Instead of trying to put white colours on a white background, it might be better to list all the physical sensations that ice, snow and frost bring. Then the spiritual sensations may be attempted if the class is advanced enough. There are hints in the 'Winter' section of the main book. In this way, the colour white will be emotion-associated rather than object-associated as autumn was.

| 30 BASIC WHITES | 30 ADVANCED WHITES | 30 GREYS |
|---|---|---|
| ang_l-white | alb_ta-white | a_h-grey |
| Ar_tic-white | albi_o-white | arg_l-grey |
| ble_ch-white | album_n-white | ceno_aph-grey |
| b_ne-white | aldr_n-white | cin_er-grey |
| dou_h-white | arc_an_el-white | cl_y-grey |
| d_ve-white | belu_a-white | fli_t-grey |
| fa_g-white | bleac_ed-b_ne white | go_se-grey |
| flo_r-white | cadav_r_us-white | gr_te-grey |
| go_se-white | calc_te-white | gra_ite-grey |
| hai_st_ne-white | cali_o-white | gra_el-grey |
| ha_o-white | cryst_l_ine-white | gra_est_ne-grey |
| l_ce-white | egr_t-white | gr_t-grey |
| mar_le-white | ermi_e-white | gri_zled-grey |
| o_b-white | gla_r-white | hi_l-mi_t-grey |
| orc_id-white | jasm_ne-white | ir_n-grey |
| o_ster-white | narw_al-white | le_d-grey |
| phan_om-white | nimb_s-white | l_am-grey |
| pol_r-white | orc_id-white | lup_ne-grey |
| por_el_in-white | pas_y-white | mana_le-grey |
| po_d_r-white | a po_ar, i_e-white | pach_derm-grey |
| pu_ty-white | prist_ne-white | pum_ce-grey |
| sea_h_ll-white | qu_ckli_e-white | sep_lchre-grey |

| | | |
|---|---|---|
| s_ull-white | sca_lop-white | sha_e-grey |
| sno_dr_p-white | tal_ow-white | smo_e-grey |
| sn_wfl_ke-white | tru_f_e-white | spec_re-grey |
| sw_n-white | tu_t-cl_ud-white | tomb_to_e-grey |
| uni_orn-white | valk_y_ie-white | und_ad-grey |
| va_p_re-white | wha_eb_ne-white | wayf_r_r-grey |
| w_n-white | wh_y-white | wer_w_lf-grey |
| a w_nt_r's-mo_n white | z_m_ie-white | zircon_um-grey |
| TOTAL= | TOTAL= | TOTAL= |

# MONSTERS

## ANIMAL EYES

| 1 Point | 2 Points | 3 Points | 4 Points | 5 Points | TOTAL |
|---------|----------|----------|----------|----------|-------|
| feli_e/ c_t | lupi_e/ wo_f | vulp__e/ fox | sim__n/ go_i__a | ang___e/ s___e | |
| serp__tine/ sn_ke | leo__ne/ lion | tau__ne /bu__ | sau__an/ li__rd | arac____/ sp___r | |

1.

2.

## EVIL EYES                                    TOTAL

| bla__ng with ang_r | fla__ing with cr__lty | gli___ng with vio_e__e | si__ring with sp__e | sc__ch__g with od___ | |
|--------------------|----------------------|------------------------|---------------------|----------------------|---|
| fla__ng with hat_ed | gl__ming with cu__ing | gli____ing with ho__i_it_ | sh___ng with ma__ce | smo__d___ng with ve__e_n__ | |

1.

2.

## COLD EYES                                    TOTAL

| fr_sty eyes | chi__ing eyes | Coss__k- cold eyes | tun__a- cold eyes | al__d eyes | |
|-------------|---------------|--------------------|--------------------|-----------|---|
| wint_y eyes | gla__al eyes | cada__r- cold eyes | fr__id eyes | ge__d eyes | |

1.

2.

## A HEARTLESS VOICE                            TOTAL

| a gr_ve | a va__t | a buri__ cham__r | a sepu_c_r_ | an oss___y | |
|---------|---------|------------------|-------------|-----------|---|
| a t_mb | a cry_t | a barr__ | a sar_op__g_s | a mau_o__u_ | |

*Writing with Stardust*

1.

2.

## A SNAKY VOICE     TOTAL

| an oi_y voice | a sl__k voice | for_-ton___d | a wheed_ing voice | an ingr__i__i_g | |
|---|---|---|---|---|---|
| a gre_sy voice | a faw__ng voice | ho__y-ton___d | a toad_ing voice | a sn__e-o_l sal__ma_'s voice | |

1.

2.

## OTHER FEATURES     TOTAL

| thi_, blo_dle_s li_s | ju_ea_s | hat__et ha_d han_s | p_p e__s and a sa__y be__d | a de___'s he__t | |
|---|---|---|---|---|---|
| raz_r-thi_ li_s | tank_rd hand_e ea_s | call___d, kno__y fi___rs | fren__ed e__s and spi__le-fle__ed l__s | a fa___w s__l | |

1.

2.

## NOSE     TOTAL

| a haw_ish nose | vult__ous | co_-n___d | pu_-n___d | a rav__'s n__e, ho___d and cr__l | |
|---|---|---|---|---|---|
| hoo_-no__d | barb__ous | bul___s | sn_b-n___d | a wi___'s, cr___ed n__e | |

1.

2.

## HAIR                                                                    TOTAL

| lif_le_s hair | gre__y hair | mat__d hair | lic_-inf___ed | pest__e_t | |
|---|---|---|---|---|---|
| lan_ hair | gri_y hair | kno__ed hair | lust_e__ss | ole_g____s | |

1.

2.

## MOCKING GRINS                                                           TOTAL

| a smi_k | a sl_l__k | a le_r | a lo_si__d g__n | a cond__c__g g__n | |
|---|---|---|---|---|---|
| a sne_r | a scor__ul l__k | a taun___g l__k | a go___n g__n | a sard___c sm__e | |

1.

2.

## STRENGTH                                                                TOTAL

| a bu__'s ne_k | a cav___n's sho__d__s | dem___c po__r | Sam___'s str__g_h | Nea_d__t_l mu___es | |
|---|---|---|---|---|---|
| a buf__lo's ne_k | a gor____'s sho__d__s | a Ti___'s po__r | Gol____'s str__g_h | a tro__o__t_'s mu__es | |

1.

2.

# BLACKS AND SPARKLING SILVERS

The most effective combination of colours is using black, red and silver together. Underneath the main grid is the type of planning grid a teacher or parent should encourage a student to make up. It may contain the images, the sounds, the sensations and the smells of a battle also if that is required. Making out these grids are the most effective way of planning a scene. They are quick, easy and fun to use. The levels can be changed according to the student's ability.

| 30 basic blacks | 30 avanced blacks | 30 sparkling silvers |
|---|---|---|
| aby_s-black | ap_cal_p_e-black | alum_n_um-silver |
| basa_t-black | Arma_e_don-black | arg_nt-silver |
| b_t-black | Bara_bas-black | bery_l_um-silver |
| c_t-black | Bee_ze_ub-black | bub_le-silver |
| c_ve-black | benz_ne-black | chai_ma_l-silver |
| cel_ar-black | bi_um_n-black | chry_a_is-silver |
| coba_t-black | blasp_em_us-black | d_w-gli_t silver |
| cob_a-black | carn_l-black | diamo_d-fl_me silver |
| cor_l-black | carr_on-black | drag_n-sc_le silver |
| corb_e-black | ca_l_ron-black | fraz_l-silver |
| co_l-black        hood | cau_k-black | gli_t_r-silver |
| de_il's-clo_k black | Char_n-black | hoa_fro_t-silver |
| de_il's-hea_t black | clo_en-ho_f black | i_e-silver |
| de_il's-so_l black | coba_t-black | me_e-silver        lake |
| do_m-black | cordi_e-black | mo_n-gl_w silver |
| ebo_y-black | cov_n-black | nic_le-silver |
| gun_ow_er-black | dama_k-black | orr_s-silver |
| ko_l-black | dam_a_ion-black | plat_n_m-silver |
| mam_a-black        snake | glo_s-black | sa_mon-silver |
| m_w-black | heat_en-black | sard_ne-silver |
| mi_nig_t-black | Ju_as-black | sea-cr_st silver |
| rav_n-black | obsi_i_n-black | sl_p_er-of-fa_ry silver |

| | | |
|---|---|---|
| pant_er-black | pag_n-black | sta_sp_rk-silver |
| sab_e-black | penta_ost_l-black | sky_ine-silver |
| scare_r_w-black | profa_e-black | spa_gle-silver |
| t_r-black | Stygi_n-black | su_erno_a-silver |
| th_n_ercl_ud-black | suc_ub_s-black | su_f-silver |
| to_d-black | vulca_i_e-black | sylv_n-silver |
| ve_v_t-black | warl_ck-black | whi_lpo_l-silver |
| wit_h-so_l black | wa_mo_ger-black | yttri_m-silver |
| TOTAL= | TOTAL= | TOTAL= |

## PLANNING A BATTLE SCENE GRID

| | | | | |
|---|---|---|---|---|
| rose-red blood | skin-crawling | crashing sounds | chrysalis-silver | wintry eyes |
| lifeless hair | coppery taste | sunless sky | blood spurting | tomb-black |
| smoky smells | arrows fizzing | eye-popping | wailing/snarling | clinking armour |

## MAKE YOUR OWN

| | | | | |
|---|---|---|---|---|
| | | | | |
| | | | | |
| | | | | |

# THE DESERT

## COLOUR

| 1 Point | 2 Points | 3 Points | 4 Points | 5 Points | TOTAL |
|---------|----------|----------|----------|----------|-------|
| bar_en-brown | scor__ed-brown | fal__w-brown | was__l_nd-brown | bu__t-um__r | |
| blas_ed-brown | sin__d-brown | fus_o_s-brown | wi_d-sco___d brown | bu__t-si___a | |

1.

2.

## SOUND TOTAL

| | | | | | |
|---|---|---|---|---|---|
| sne_k_ng | scr___ling | scra___ing | sli___ring | sid___g | |
| scr_p_ng | scraw__ng | scra__ling | slin__ng | sku__ing | |

1.

2.

## INACTION TOTAL

| | | | | | |
|---|---|---|---|---|---|
| em_ty | ar__ | des_i__ted | feat__l_s | ste__e | |
| life__ss | bar__n | des__a_e | for__n | je__n_ | |

1.

2.

## METAPHORS TOTAL

| | | | | | |
|---|---|---|---|---|---|
| the de__l's gar__n | Sa__n's sa_na | Luc___r's ga__n | the d____'s cau__n | Aba__on's arb_r__um | |
| Ol_ Nic_'s oven | Sa__n's sa_na | Luc___r's gr__l | the d____'s cre_a_o___m | Bee_z__ub's ba__ho_e | |

1.

2.

## ANIMALS OF THE DESERT                              TOTAL

| ca__l | de___t li__ | de__t f__ | sc__io__ | ta__n__l | |
|---|---|---|---|---|---|
| li__rd | bo__at | co___e | ra___es___e | va___e b__ | |

1.

2.

## PLANTS OF THE DESERT                              TOTAL

| ca__us | brit__e bush | jump__g cholla | panc__e ca__us | de___T iro__w__d | |
|---|---|---|---|---|---|
| soa__tre_ | cha__n frui_ | ocoti__lo | creo__te bush | Jos__a tree | |

1.

2.

## BIRDS OF THE DESERT                              TOTAL

| cr_w | ea__e | hu____g b__d | ca___s wr__ | ro__ru___r | |
|---|---|---|---|---|---|
| o_l | ha_k | de__t qua_l | ca___s w__dpe___r | v____e | |

1.

2.

## SMELL                              TOTAL

| bur_ed and bla_ted | ba__d and ba_b__u_d | gri___ed and gr___ed | sco___d and sea__d | sim____d and ske_e__d | |
|---|---|---|---|---|---|
| fla_ed and fri_d | bla_ed and bl__ed | roa___d and sau___d | comb____d and co___d | si__l_d and to___d | |

1.

2.

## SENSATION                                                          TOTAL

| a dr_,gri_ty mouth | swo__en ton__e | par__ed th__t | fee_ like h__ co__s | sk__ scr___d by sa__pa__r | |
|---|---|---|---|---|---|
| swe_t sod_en | brai_ infl__ed | deh_d___ed li__r | fa_e like Gr__k f__e | sk__ st___ed by s__-sp__rs | |

1.

2.

## TASTE                                                              TOTAL

| joy_ess taste | jui__less taste | lis__ess taste | va__d taste | maw___h taste | |
|---|---|---|---|---|---|
| tas_eless | spir___ess taste | savo___ess taste | ins__d taste | wer__ taste | |

1.

2.

# PURPLES, ORANGES AND PINKS

One of the most effective techniques to use with a class of students is to pluck out words from the grids and use them verbally in a story. For example, the educator might start with the sentence: "The desert was a blasted-brown colour". The student might then respond with: "The scraping sound of a desert rodent was annoying". The story may be developed using this technique. It can be done with an individual or a group. When the words from the grids are used up, just let imagination take over and keep the story moving. The importance of a plot and introducing characters such as nomads and encountering other lost adventurers can be very rewarding. Are the eyes of the nomads Berber-brown? What type of clothes are they wearing? Are they hostile or friendly characters? If a term was to be applied to this exercise, it might be 'chain narration'. The story keeps moving, prompted by the educator in question. It gives the student ownership of the story, but doesn't dent their confidence by working in a vacuum of ideas. If it attempted with a group of students it will be more successful. You will be amazed how they flourish and seek to outdo each other with creative ideas. The important aspect of it is to have a list of words pre-arranged. Once the students get used to this, the safety valve of having to use word banks may be taken away.

| 20 purples | 20 oranges | 20 pinks |
|---|---|---|
| amethy_t-purple | amb_r-orange | blos_om-pink |
| b_rd-of-par_d_se purple | aureol_n-orange | a blu_hing, pilg_im-pink |
| bis_op's mit_e-purple | blaz_ng-orange | calam_ne-pink |
| gridel_n-purple | b_iling-orange | cand_fl_ss-pink |
| heath_r-purple | bro_ling-orange | ceri_e-pink |
| indi_o-purple | bur_ing-orange | da_n-pink |
| junip_r-purple | emb_r-orange | diam_nd-pink |
| laven_er-purple | glo_ing-orange | dus_y-pink |
| lil_c-purple | fev_rish-orange | flam_n_o-pink |
| magen_a-purple | fi_ry-orange | fle_h-pink |
| mau_e-purple | h_t-orange | fuch_ia-pink |
| monar_hy-purple | nacar_t-orange | peo_y-pink |

| | | |
|---|---|---|
| mulbe_ry-purple | och_e-orange | pet_l-pink |
| orpi_e-purple | scorc_ing-orange | pra_n-pink |
| p_aco_k-purple | smou_de_ing-orange | ro_e-pink |
| pl_m-purple | sun_et-orange | ro_epet_l-pink |
| pru_e-purple | swel_ering-orange | sa_mon-pink |
| ro_al-purple | tang_r_ne-orange | sorb_t-pink |
| Tyri_n-purple | tig_r str_pe-orange | su_ri_e-pink |
| vio_et-purple | vulpi_e-orange | orc_id-pink |
| TOTAL= | TOTAL= | TOTAL= |

# BATTLE SCENES

## SKY COLOUR

| 1 Point | 2 Points | 3 Points | 4 Points | 5 Points | TOTAL |
|---|---|---|---|---|---|
| ba_-black | cau__ro_-black | pag__-black | cor__e-black | Bar___as-black | |
| cob_a-black | car__on-black | prof__e-black | car__l-black | Be_lz__ub-black | |

1.

2.

## BLOOD COLOUR     TOTAL

| ber_y-red | po__y-red | ma__a-red | bal_f__e-red | hel_a_i__s-red | |
|---|---|---|---|---|---|
| merc_ry-red | bra_i_r-red | mol__n-red | bri_st__e-red | Ti_i_n-red | |

1.

2.

## BATTLE SOUNDS     TOTAL

| ba_ging and ba_hing | clo__ering and clu__ing | sma__ing and sm_t_ng | car___g and cle___ng | ha____g and he___g | |
|---|---|---|---|---|---|
| batt__ing and bea_ing | clun__ng and cra__ing | pou___ng and pu_m___ing | bla___g and blu__e_n__g | la__ing/ga__ing and man__ing/go__ing | |

1.

2.

## MISSILE SOUNDS     TOTAL

| buz_ing and fiz_ing | shr__ling and sis__ng | pu_ing and pur_ing | tre_b__ng and thr_m__ng | ski_l__g and si__l__g | |
|---|---|---|---|---|---|
| fi_zling friz_ling | zip__ng his__ng | ras__ng kee__ng | whi__ing whi__ling | whi___g wai___g | |

1.

2.

## CRIES OF PAIN

TOTAL

| scre_ming and scre_ching | sna__ing and sq_e_ling | ro__ing and mew__g | gro____g and yow__g | ba__ing and be__o___g | |
|---|---|---|---|---|---|
| wai_ing and whim_ering | so__ing and sn_v_l_ing | blu_b__ing and cho___g | yel___g and ya_m__ing | ke__ing and ca_e_w__ling | |

1.

2.

## SOUNDS OF METAL

TOTAL

| ch_ming | cli__ing | ji__ing | cla__ering | cl___ing | |
|---|---|---|---|---|---|
| chi_king | ri__ing | ja__ing | cla_k__g | cla__o_r__s | |

1.

2.

## PLURAL NOUNS FOR MONSTERS

TOTAL

| a se__of ene__ies | a fl__d of mo__t_rs | a ho_t of og__s | a hi_e of ca__ib_s | a pl___e of he__ho__ds | |
|---|---|---|---|---|---|
| a swa_m of op_on_nts | a le_i_n of tr__ls | a ho_e of be__ts | a thr__g of go__i_s | an inf_ta__on of or__ | |

1.

2.

## SMELL

TOTAL

| vil_ | si_kly | nox___s | pun__nt | mil_e_y | |
|---|---|---|---|---|---|
| ung_dly | sep_ic | naus___ng | putr_f__ng | mor__t | |

1.

2.

## SENSATION                                                                          TOTAL

| ey_-<br>po_ping | hea_-<br>clas_ing | sk__-<br>cr_ling | bo__-<br>rat____g | bla___r-<br>emp___ng | |
|---|---|---|---|---|---|
| hea_t-<br>th_mping | mar_ow-<br>fre__ing | spi_e-<br>chi__ing | bl__d-<br>cur___ng | bo__l-<br>lo_s__i_g | |

1.

2.

## TASTE                                                                                   TOTAL

| sa_ty | acr_d | ta__y | bra__ish | cer__ean | |
|---|---|---|---|---|---|
| sali_e | vine_ary | ta_t | br__y | co__ery | |

1.

2.

# TEACHING ABOUT TEXTURE

The dictionary definition of texture: "The feel or appearance of a surface or substance". Personally, I prefer to use a simpler definition with my students. I would argue that it is **a sensation that comes with a specific image.** If one can't feel it as well as visualise it, then it is what I call texture-neutral. For example, let us look at the words 'boggy' and 'squelchy'. If you describe something as boggy, it should give the sensation of a foot stepping into a puddle in a bog. This is very specific. The word 'bog' is a noun and it helps to form a concrete image. Although 'squelchy' is very effective, you can't touch a squelch! Therefore, it gives a sensation but not a **specific image.** It is not a texture because it doesn't have a surface. That is the next part of the definition. If you can't touch it with your fingertip, dismiss it as a texture for descriptive writing purposes. The same applies for the words 'hot' and 'hob-hot'. The difference is huge. Try placing your finger on a hot hob and you will get both the texture and a stinging sensation! The texture is hard and the sensation is hot. Try to avoid all such experiments! It is easier to use a definition of texture that keeps it simple for students. Underneath is a grid to help educators understand the differences. Try to figure out why 'icy' and 'frosty' are textures, but 'frozen' is not.

## TEXTURES

| Noun/image | Soft/wet texture | Noun/image | Non-soft texture | Texture-neutral |
|---|---|---|---|---|
| bog | **boggy** | barb | **barbed** | coarse |
| bubble | **bubbly** | crust | **crusty** | cold |
| butter | **buttery** | enamel | **enamelled** | delicate |
| cream | **creamy** | flint | **flinty** | finespun |
| dough | **doughy** | frost | **frosty** | frozen |
| eiderdown | **downy** | glass | **glassy** | hot |
| feather | **feathery** | grain | **grainy** | rich |
| fleece | **fleecy** | gravel | **gravelly** | rough |
| fluff | **fluffy** | grime | **grimy** | smooth |
| foam | **foamy** | grit | **gritty** | solid |
| gauze | **gauzy** | hob | **hob-hot** | |
| gossamer | **gossamery** | ice | **icy** | |

| hair | **hairy** | leather | **leathery** | |
| honey | **honeyed** | lacquer | **lacquered** | |
| satin | **satin-soft** | metal | **metallic** | |
| silk | **silky** | polish | **polished** | |
| sponge | **spongy** | rock | **rocky** | |
| velvet | **velvety** | stone | **stony** | |
| wax | **waxy** | stubble | **stubbly** | |
| wool | **wooly** | wood | **woody** | |

The adjectives can be used in all the chapters in the book. They can be used for the grass, armour, sand, skin, hair and so many more. It always adds a 'punch' to an essay if a student can describe the exact texture he/she is experiencing. Like the effect of onomatopoeia, it catapults the reader into the world of the writer. The best way to approach the teaching of texture is to blindfold the students. Place different objects for them to touch and provide an adjective for. It is very educational and it is always a fun-filled session.

# MIST: RAIN: FLOOD RIVERS

## COLOUR

| 1 Point | 2 Points | 3 Points | 4 Points | 5 Points | TOTAL |
|---|---|---|---|---|---|
| gho_t-grey | sp_ok-grey | phan__m-grey | phan__sm-grey | wr___h-grey | |
| gho_l-grey | spec__e-grey | polt_g__st-grey | fan__sm-grey | a_p__i_i_n | |

1.

2.

## LACK OF SOUND                                  TOTAL

| | | | | | |
|---|---|---|---|---|---|
| voic_less and hear_less | wo__less and pa__io_less | ton__eless and spi__less | so___less and sou__ess | fa_h__less and fri___less | |
| nois_less and blo_dless | li__less and mo__erless | ro__less and bre__hless | ec__less and emo_i__less | ki_less and ki__less | |

1.

2.

## SHAPE                                  TOTAL

| | | | | | |
|---|---|---|---|---|---|
| shr_ds | r_gs | ten___les | fin__rs | mem_r__es | |
| shav_ngs | ri__ons | tas__ls | fet__s | mi__m_s | |

1.

2.

## ACTION                                    TOTAL

| sm_ky and ste_ming | fu_y and fil_y | sorc__ous and ill__ory | evane_c__t and ephe_e__l | bru___s and neb__ous | |
|---|---|---|---|---|---|
| tran_e-like and mir_ge-like | ha_y and gau_y | ethe_e_l and gos_a_er-frag__e | vapo_o_s and diap_o_o_s | unea___ly and oth__w__l_ly | |

1.

2.

## RAIN SOUNDS                              TOTAL

| spr_ying | sussu__ting | spi__ing | shre__ing | si__l__g | |
|---|---|---|---|---|---|
| show_ring | sis_ing | sibi__nt | se_t_ing | slu___g | |

1.

2.

## LIGHT RAIN                               TOTAL

| a_ry rain | mis_-like | dro___ts of | de_dr__s of | dri__l__g rain | |
|---|---|---|---|---|---|
| aerif_rm | spri___ing | pe__ls of | tea__r__s of | mi__l__g rain | |

1.

2.

## HEAVY RAIN                               TOTAL

| plu_p dro_s of | swo_l_n dro_s of | soa_ing rain | i_y rain | si__er na__s of | |
|---|---|---|---|---|---|
| plo_py dro_s of | pre_n_nt dro_s of | sat_a_ing rain | sti__ing rain | si__er bu__e_s of | |

1.

2.

## FLOODED RIVER COLOURS                                  TOTAL

| t_a-brown and boi_ing | whis__y-brown and slo__ing | bra__y-brown and roi_ing | cog__c-brown and fo__ing | mo__a-brown and lat__ring | |
|---|---|---|---|---|---|
| b_g-brown and broi_ing | tu_f-brown and slu__ing | pe_t-brown and rum__ing | est__ry-brown and fr__hy | mol__s_s-brown and th_e__ing | |

1.

2.

# TEACHING A SPORTS ESSAY

Who among us hasn't gotten the claustrophobic, lung-burning smell of cheap anti-perspirant in the dressing room? Who hasn't had their nostrils invaded by the steaming, sweaty smell of mildewed jerseys as they stew away in the corner? Who hasn't marked an opponent who left a vapour trail of afterburn behind him as he raced for the goal? Apparently, our students haven't! Every time I assign a sports essay, the start, beginning and the end are the same. It's like that Latin quote: "veni, vidi, vici" (we came, we saw, we conquered). It never ceases to amaze me how similar the sports essays have been from a multitude of different students. Sometimes I ask with genuine bafflement: "Do you ever lose?!" The answer to that is the same also: "What kind of story are you asking us to write?" In an attempt to combat this and provide VARIETY in the sports essay, I will provide a template for ideas that may inspire some creativity. It is not an end in itself, but it might help.

| LEVEL 1 | LEVEL 2 | LEVEL 3 | LEVEL 4 | LEVEL 5 |
|---------|---------|---------|---------|---------|

### DEMONISING YOUR OPPONENT

| cave trolls from a fable | filed-down fangs | beady, glinting eyes | ghouls from a horror movie | serial killer mentality |
|---------|---------|---------|---------|---------|
| knuckles scraping the ground | broken-glass teeth | bulbous, bulging eyes | monsters from a gore-fest | dead-fish eyes |

### STORMY METAPHORS

| a tornado of sound | a blizzard of scores | a cyclone of sound | a geyser of anger | a tsunami of noise |
|---------|---------|---------|---------|---------|
| a hurricane of passion | a whirlpool of rage | a volcano of noise | a tempest of tackles | a vortex of emotions |

## CREATING ATMOSPHERE

| bangers exploded | fireworks whizzed | firecrackers detonated | rockets whooshed | thunderflashes blinded us |
|---|---|---|---|---|
| crackers popped | flares sizzled | sparklers sizzed | squibs hissed | drums like the roll of doom |

## THE CROWD GO SILENT

| convent quiet | tomb quiet | vault silent | catacomb silent | sacristy silent |
|---|---|---|---|---|
| cathedral quiet | vow quiet | vigil silent | cenotaph silent | amniotic silent |

## LOSING THE GAME ( YES-LOSING!)

| cut to pieces | ants walking in treacle | lambs against ravenous wolves | mangled and mutilated | garrotted and gelded |
|---|---|---|---|---|
| cut to ribbons | shredded like tissue paper | powder-puff defending | ground down like bruxism | eviscerated and euthanised |

## SLOW ATHLETES

| snail slow | turtle slow | sloth slow | leaden footed | bovine slow |
|---|---|---|---|---|
| slug slow | tortoise slow | slug-a-bed slow | lawnmower slow | laggard slow |

## FAST ATHLETES

| TURBO | SUBSONIC | SUPERSONIC | MACH 9 | WARP 9 |
|---|---|---|---|---|
| lightning fast | greyhound-heeled | rocket fast | Concorde-heeled | exocet-heeled |
| jet heeled | star blaze fast | quicksilver fast | booster-heeled | will-o'-the-wisp fast |

## THE MOTION OF THE BALL

| | | | | |
|---|---|---|---|---|
| flew and floated | skimmed and screamed | fizzed and flashed in the air | arrowed and arced | whizzed and whined |
| soared and sailed | hung and hovered | hummed and hurtled | whipped and whirred | zipped and zoomed |

## OTHER IMAGES

| | | | | |
|---|---|---|---|---|
| burger stands | dew gleaming like fallen stars | neon lights of the scoreboard | lush-green sward of pitch | a kaleidoscope of colour |
| ambulances waiting | puce-faced referee | crowd giving the thumbs-down | fluorescent-jacketed steward | a pageantry of colour |

## DRESSING ROOM SMELLS

| | | | | |
|---|---|---|---|---|
| a musty soup of stale air and old smells | a potent cocktail of body odour and urine | the casualty ward odour of bandages and blood | the malodorous pong of cheap after shave and armpits | the putrefying odour of vomit and empty bladders |
| the clinical smell of bleach and disinfectant | a toxic pong of old socks and sweat | a mordant stew of mildewed jerseys and man-smells | the mephitic nip of chlorine and disinfectant | the pungent, noxious smell of defeat |

If nothing else, the dressing room smells should get the attention of whoever is reading it!

# THUNDER AND LIGHTNING

## COLOUR

| 1 Point | 2 Points | 3 Points | 4 Points | 5 Points | TOTAL |
|---|---|---|---|---|---|
| ra_en-black | cow_-black | wit__-so_l black | ab__s-black | hea__en-black | |
| mam_a-black | cov_n-black | de__l-he__t black | suc_u__s-black | bla__h_m__s-black | |

1.

2.

## SOUND                                             TOTAL

| boo_ing and blas_ing | cla__ing and bel__wing | gr__ning and gr__ling | ro____g and ro__ing | son__o_s and ste_t_r__n | |
|---|---|---|---|---|---|
| clan_ing and cla_king | cra_king and cra__ing | gr__bling and ru__ing | pe__ing and yo__ing | cac__h__ous and cla__o_ous | |

1.

2.

## SHAPE                                             TOTAL

| boi_ing skies | rio_ous skies | cru__ling skies | mo__ing skies | tur_____t skies | |
|---|---|---|---|---|---|
| chur_ing skies | rum_led skies | bu__ling skies | ro__ing skies | tum__t__us skies | |

1.

2.

## ACTION                                          TOTAL

| explos_on | ra_g | mou__ful | res__a__d | so__re |  |
|---|---|---|---|---|---|
| det_nat_on | ech__d | disc__dant | rev__be__t_d | so__c b__m |  |

1.

2.

## LIGHTNING COLOUR                                TOTAL

| st_r fl-me-gold | lus__o-s-gold | gli__r-gold | f__l-gold | ga_li__t-gold |  |
|---|---|---|---|---|---|
| st_r bl_ze-gold | lum__o_s-gold | gam__ge-gold | ful__us-gold | G__-go__e_ed |  |

1.

2.

## SOUND                                           TOTAL

| bu_zed | hi__ed | fi__ed | sco___ed | whi__d |  |
|---|---|---|---|---|---|
| crac_led | si__ed | fi__led | sea__d | si__d |  |

1.

2.

## SHAPE                                           TOTAL

| bra_ched | pr__ged | cr__ed | ant__ed | den__i__rm |  |
|---|---|---|---|---|---|
| for_ed | vei__d | con__ted | spl__d | bif__a_ed |  |

1.

2.

## ACTION                                          TOTAL

| bla_ing | hu__ng | whi_ing | sla_ing | ra__ng |  |
|---|---|---|---|---|---|
| pu_ring | qui_er__g | wri__ing | sq___ing | z__a_ing |  |

1.

2.

## COLD SEAS                                    TOTAL

| a co_d, st_el-blue | an ic_, pol_r-blue | a chi___ng, Sib___an-blue | alp__e-blue and al__d | Ant_____c-blue and fr___d | |
|---|---|---|---|---|---|
| a co_d, wint_y-blue | an icy, Pru___an-blue | ar___c-blue and cor__e-cold | ice___g-blue and Co___ck-cold | gl____r-blue and g___d | |

1.

2.

## ANGRY SEAS                                   TOTAL

| bas__ng the roc_s | sma__ing the cl___s | bu__eting the co__t | sp__ing sp__e | wh__s_ing w___s | |
|---|---|---|---|---|---|
| bat_ering the roc_s | sm_s_ing the cl___s | blu__e_ning the co__t | sup_u_a__ng ha__ed | wa__o__ng w___s | |

1.

2.

# NG A YEARLY PLANNER

cide the level of ability of the class/student and plan
ordingly. The point to be made is that a student should not be introduced to another
n literary device without first having mastered the definition and use of the previous one.
quence for introducing terms is highlighted in bold.

## LEVEL 1

1. Rivers and Streams: Colour, Sound, Shape, Action, Sensation, Smell, Taste.

2. Mountains: Colour, Sound, Shape, Action, **Imagery**, Sensation, Smell, Taste.

3. The Beach: Colour, Sound, Shape, **Metaphors**, Sensation, Smell, Taste.

4. Waterfalls: Colour, **Soft Sounds, Loud Sounds**, Action, Sensation, Smell, Taste.

5. The Forest: Colour, Sound, Shape of Stars, Metaphors, **Animals and Plants**, etc.

## LEVEL 2

1. Rivers and Streams: As above: Introduce **Similes**.

2. Mountains: As above: Introduce **Pathetic Fallacy**.

3. The Beach: As Above: Introduce **Onomatopoeia**.

4. Waterfalls: As Above: Introduce **Euphony** through p.49 grid of main book.

5. The Forest: As Above: Introduce **Alliteration**.

## LEVEL 3

1. The Desert: Introduce **'Painting in a Blank Canvas'** (i.e the writer as a painter filling in detail).

2. Spring: Introduce **Assonance** and how each season has a unique soul a writer must capture.

3. Summer: Introduce **'Zoom Narration'** and apply it to a feature of summer (a beach etc.)

4. Autumn: Introduce **Archaic Words** and their ability to transform a text.

5. Winter: Introduce **Cacaphony** and the difference between the internal/ external world.

## LEVEL 4

1. Mist and Rain: Introduce **Sibilance** and how the mist and rain can transform an essay.

2. Thunder and Lightning: Introduce the **Level 4 Formula** as an example of pattern in nature.

3. Describing Monsters: Introduce how to **demonize** a character and how it can be fun!

4. Describing Females: Introduce how to **eulogise** a character and attention to detail.

5. Describing Males: Introduce the **'mock-heroic'** qualities (Apollo biceps etc.).

# TEACHING A YEARLY PLANNER

## LEVEL 5

These essays are where all the skills learned in the previous chapters blend together. They also allow for a wide variety of writing styles and genres. Listed below are some of the most important techniques that should be developed in a student.

## ESSAY TECHNIQUES

1. The **'narrative voice'** must be decided first of all. Shall it be in the first person, second person, omniscient format or a mixture of these?

2. Exploring **'universal themes'** is advisable at this level. Examples may include: fear, bravery, guilt, loyalty, death, cowardice and glory.

3. Constructing a **credible plot** is very important. This should be pre-planned and not written 'on the hoof', as they say.

4. Organising strong and **structured paragraphs** is essential. This will ensure that there is fluency and a flow to the essay.

5. Establishing **interesting characters** is vital. The amount of characters, both the main character and the fringe characters, should be planned in advance also.

6. Is the main character a hero/heroine or an **anti-hero**? Is he a noble man forced to commit acts of violence or is he a bad man who chooses/ is forced to commit noble deeds?

7. Is a **'stream-of–consciousness'** technique going to be used? Are we, as readers, going to get an insight into the private, innermost thoughts of the main character?

8. Is the **atmosphere/mood** going to capture the spirit of the essay title? Can the student construct a world suitable for the genre?

9. Will there be a **variety of syntax**? Does the student have the ability to consciously shorten some sentences for dramatic effect? Shall rhetorical questions be used?

10. May we, as readers, expect a **'flashback technique'** to be adopted in some cases? This might be diary entries or just a trip down memory lane to a happier time for the hero/heroine.


## LEVEL 5 SUGGESTIONS

1. Describing Battle Scenes: Develop the concept of **universal themes**.

2. The Dark Forest: Develop the concept of the **anti-hero** and the **fable/fantasy genre** (like the gothic genre of the Grimm brothers, for example.)

3. The Sports Essay: Develop the concept of **atmosphere** in a story.

4. Adrift At Sea: Develop the concept of **stream-of-consciousness** in a dying man.

5. Alone in the Arctic: Develop the **flashback technique** in diary or essay form.

# THE DARK FOREST

## COLOUR

| 1 Point | 2 Points | 3 Points | 4 Points | 5 Points | TOTAL |
|---------|----------|----------|----------|----------|-------|
| bi_e-brown | tox_c-brown | mot__ed-brown | bl__c_ed-brown | phl__m-brown | |
| blad_er-brown | nicot__e-brown | mala_y-brown | brin__ed-brown | sp_t_m-brown | |

1.

2.

## A MONSTERS FEAST      TOTAL

| | | | | | |
|---|---|---|---|---|---|
| che_ing and chom_ing tr__ls | gna_ing and gna_hing og__s | slu__ing and slo___ring va___es | gu__ling and guz__ing ho_g__l ns | mun____g and mas___a__g ca_i__s | |
| cham_ing and crun_hing wit__es | gob__ing and gri__ing di_e wo__es | sme__ing and sal_v__ing gh__ls | dr__bling and dr___l__ng ni__t wa___rs | qu___ing and wal____g rev_n__ts | |

1.

2.

## DARK WOODS      TOTAL

| | | | | | |
|---|---|---|---|---|---|
| sha_y gla_es | gl__my sc_u_s | sun_e_s cop__s | du__y wea_ds | ful_g_n__s ho__s | |
| sha_owy gro_es | mu__y thi___ts | soo-y cop_i_es | tur__d spi__eys | luc_f__ous hur_-s | |

1.

2.

## BAD AIR                                TOTAL

| st_le air | mus_y air | da_k air | cl___y air | fu__y air | |
| stu_fy air | mou__y air | dec__ing air | cla_st__ph__ic air | fr__sty air | |

1.

2.

## YE OLDE FORESTE                        TOTAL

| ancestr_l | oth__w__ldly | prim__al | ar___e | eld___c_ | |
| antiqua_ed | unea___ly | prim__d__l | atav___c | prete__a_u__l | |

1.

2.

## OTHER IMAGES                           TOTAL

| reac_ing and spraw_ing lim_s | thi_h-th__k cre__ers | dea_ly hel_eb__e slu__ing the nutr__n_s | sty_ian-bl__k str__ms and sy__p-sl_w | cob__bs shi____ing like mes__d st_l | |
| trees glar_ng like sil_nt sentr_es | oxb__d-red to__st___s | mo__led bar_like fro_en so_p | clo__s of ca__on__ll-bl__k fl__s | pest__en_ st__m like spo__y inc__se | |

1.

2.

## FOREST POISONS                         TOTAL

| fo_l's pars_ey | cuc_oo pi_t | lar_sp_r | dea__y nig__sh__e | he__eb__e | |
| wol_s bane | cowb__e | pant__r c_p | de__s bol_t_ | he__oc_ | |

1.

2.

## SMELL

| | | | | | TOTAL |
|---|---|---|---|---|---|
| mu_ty sm_ll | acr_d od__r | ra_k mia__a | to_ic re_k | ra___d | |
| yu_ky p__g | fet_d st__ch | pun__nt ta_g | t__t eme_at__n | mep_i__c n_p | |

1.

2.

## SENSATION

| | | | | | TOTAL |
|---|---|---|---|---|---|
| ha_r-rai_ing | tee_h-gri__ing | bl__d-chu__ing | mar__w-conge___ng | mi__-nu___g | |
| spi_e-chil_ing | thr_t-constr__ting | ve_n-fre___ng | pul_e-qui__e__ng | ni___ma__-ins_i__g | |

1.

2.

## THE TASTE OF BLOOD

| | | | | | TOTAL |
|---|---|---|---|---|---|
| oi_y taste | so_r taste | sic__n__g taste | ac___c taste | ace__ic taste | |
| fis_y taste | met_l__c taste | vam___ish taste | ca_t_c taste | astr_g__t taste | |

1.

2.

# A JUMBLE BOX OF EMOTIONS

Every essay a student attempts enables him/her to tap into the range of emotions a character may feel. Although it is wiser for diary entries to keep the diction very basic, a Level 5 essay may require emotions with 'punch'. I shall fill in some of the more basic emotions in a grid format. Underneath that is a 'jumble box' for educators to fill in words commensurate with the level of the student/class. It should be a lot of fun listening to the emotions he/she/they feel every day and to empathise with them.

## HAPPINESS

| LEVEL 1 | LEVEL 2 | LEVEL 3 | LEVEL 4 | LEVEL 5 | OTHERS |
|---------|---------|---------|---------|---------|--------|
| mer_y | del_ght_ed | jubi_a_t | ec_t_t_c | rap_ur_us | |
| jol_y | o_erj_yed | int_x_ca_ed | eup_o_ic | del_r_ous | |

## SADNESS

| LEVEL 1 | LEVEL 2 | LEVEL 3 | LEVEL 4 | LEVEL 5 | OTHERS |
|---------|---------|---------|---------|---------|--------|
| crus_ed | br_k_n hea_ted | dej_c_ed | lachr_m_se | wret_hed | |
| downhe_rted | hea_y hea_ted | dem_r_li_ed | lugu_ri_us | woe_eg_ne | |

## LONELINESS

| LEVEL 1 | LEVEL 2 | LEVEL 3 | LEVEL 4 | LEVEL 5 | OTHERS |
|---------|---------|---------|---------|---------|--------|
| lon_ly | lone_ome | a_her_it | estra_g_d | forl_rn | |
| abando_ed | iso_ated | a_pari_h | exc_m_unica_ed | fo_sa_en | |

## FEAR

| LEVEL 1 | LEVEL 2 | LEVEL 3 | LEVEL 4 | LEVEL 5 | OTHERS |
|---------|---------|---------|---------|---------|--------|
| nervo_s | an_ious | pa_ano_d | int_m_dat_d | pa_ic-stri_k_n | |
| fri_ht_ned | fea_fu_ | pa_al_sed | appr_h_ns_ve | cow_d | |

**THE 'JUMBLE BOX'**

|  |  |  |  |  |
|---|---|---|---|---|
|  |  |  |  |  |
|  |  |  | contented |  |
|  |  |  |  |  |
|  | bliss |  |  |  |
|  |  |  |  |  |
|  |  |  |  |  |
|  |  | energised |  |  |
|  |  |  |  |  |
|  |  |  |  |  |
| shame |  |  |  |  |
|  |  |  |  | guilty |
|  |  |  |  |  |

# FEMALES

## FIGURE

| 1 point | 2 point | 3 points | 4 points | 5 points | TOTAL |
|---|---|---|---|---|---|
| an hou_ glas_ figure | a scu_p_ed figure | a com__y figure | a qu___ly figure | a me__a_d's figure | |
| a shap__y figure | a svel_e figure | a curv_c__us figure | an Ama_o___n figure | a wi__o_y figure | |

1.

2.

## BODY                                                          TOTAL

| el_ -thin | wh__-thin | st_m-thin | wa__r-thin | or__a_-thin | |
|---|---|---|---|---|---|
| im_ -thin | tw__e-thin | sap___g-thin | wa_f-thin | ma__e_u__-thin | |

1.

2.

## WAIST                                                         TOTAL

| a bum_l_be_ waist | a tape_e_ waist | a cha_i_e sha_ed waist | a gob__t sha_ed waist | an ox__w waist | |
|---|---|---|---|---|---|
| wa_p-wais_ed | a syl_h-like waist | a curv_lin__r waist | a deca_t_r sha_ed waist | a y_w b_w waist | |

1.

2.

## COMPLEXION                                    TOTAL

| | | | | | |
|---|---|---|---|---|---|
| glo_ing sk_n | a bron__d compl__i_n | a citr_n ti_t | an apr_c_t hu_ | a pigm__t per___t tin_tu_e | |
| glo_sy sk_n | a burn__h_d compl__i_n | a saff__n ti_t | an och__us hu_ | a pea__es and cr__m c___le__n | |

1.

2.

## EYEBROWS                                    TOTAL

| | | | | | |
|---|---|---|---|---|---|
| slen_er eyebrows | arc__d eyebrows | cres__nt shaped eyebrows | penc__-thi_ eyebrows | qua___-m__n eyebrows | |
| plu_k_d eyebrows | cur_ed eyebrows | ecl__se shaped eyebrows | sym_e__i__l eyebrows | sli__r-o_-m__n eyebrows | |

1.

2.

## EYELASHES                                    TOTAL

| | | | | | |
|---|---|---|---|---|---|
| sil_y eyelashes | swe_p__g eyelashes | lan__id eyelashes | bee__e-l_g eyelashes | Cle_pa__a eyelashes | |
| ve_v_ty eyelashes | fi_e-sp_n eyelashes | lang__o_s eyelashes | sp__er-l_g eyelashes | Merov__g__n eyelashes | |

1.

2.

## EARS                                    TOTAL

| | | | | | |
|---|---|---|---|---|---|
| elf_n ears | delic__e ears | scro___d ears | a cher__'s ears | sea___l sh__ed ears | |
| sea nym_h ears | ethe_ea_ ears | whor__d ears | a sera__'s ears | sca___p sh__ed ears | |

1.

2.

## NOSE TOTAL

| a poi_ty nose | a butt_n nose | an ele__nt nose | a pi__e's nose | a Mus_s' nose | |
|---|---|---|---|---|---|
| a dai_ty nose | a pe_t nose | a lin__r nose | a fil_ st__'s nose | a di_a's nose | |

1.

2.

## TEETH TOTAL

| shi__ng, ha_o-white | da__ling, an__l-white | pris___e, cal__te-white | bew__ch__g, uni___n-white | flu__es___t, por__l__n-white | |
|---|---|---|---|---|---|
| gle__ing, blea_h-white | spa___ing, arch___el-white | lum___us, hea___ly-white | beg__li_g, oy___r-white | spe__bi____g, wi___d-white | |

1.

2.

## FINGERNAILS TOTAL

| var__shed | sir_n_red | fil_ st_r | Ve__s-red | pend__t sh___d | |
|---|---|---|---|---|---|
| man___red | carm__e-red | henn__d | Aph__di_e-red | sti_e_o sh___d | |

1.

2.

# CREATING 'PULSE' WORDS

It always gives me a sense of satisfaction to meet past pupils many years after they have left. Most of them like to remind me how I instilled a love of words and language into them. Quite a few will then give me examples of said words and are very proud to have remembered them! The most common is 'salubrious' (good for one's health), followed by arcipluvian (multi-coloured) and azoic (lifeless). No matter who the student is, it is great to see them have a love of words. When the students are reading 'Writing with Stardust', they should be encouraged to place their favourite colours, nouns, verbs and adjectives in the grid below. The grid is blank in order for each student to find his/her level of ability.

## BEAUTIFUL AND IMPACTFUL WORDS

| | | | | |
|---|---|---|---|---|
| | | | | |
| | | | | |
| | | | | |
| | | | | |
| | | | | |
| | | | | |
| | | | | |
| | | | | |
| | | | | |
| | | | | |
| | | | | |
| | | | | |
| | | | | |
| | | | | |
| | | | | |
| | | | | |
| | | | | |
| | | | | |
| | | | | |

# FEMALES

### RED HAIR

| 1 point | 2 points | 3 points | 4 points | 5 points | TOTAL |
|---------|----------|----------|----------|----------|-------|
| merc__y-red | ma__a-red | ru__-red | solfe___o-red | verm__l-red | |
| molt_n-red | la_a-red | rou_e-red | Ti_i_n-red | verm_l__n-red | |

1.

2.

### BLACK HAIR                                              TOTAL

| | | | | | |
|---|---|---|---|---|---|
| midn__ht-black | ko_l-black | co__l-black | sa__e-black | vulc__i_e-black | |
| ebo_y-black | mo__sha__w-black | cob__t-black | m_w-black | obs_d__n-black | |

1.

2.

### BLONDE HAIR                                             TOTAL

| | | | | | |
|---|---|---|---|---|---|
| su_r_se-gold | mo__gl__m-gold | st__fla_e-gold | o__-gold | Ar_-o_-C__en_t gold | |
| su_s_t-gold | mo__gli__-gold | st__b__m-gold | h_p str__g-gold | Val_y__e-gold | |

1.

2.

## BROWN HAIR                                      TOTAL

| lo__s of ches_n_t-brown | wis_s of aub__n-brown | tum___s of rus__t-brown | swi__s of car__el-brown | ske__s of cop__r-brown | |
|---|---|---|---|---|---|
| co_ls of le_f-brown | ri__l_ts of ta__y-brown | tre___s of mo__y-brown | spo__s of nou__t-brown | Rest__a__on cu__s of cin_a_o_-brown | |

1.

2.

## COLOUR OF EYES                                 TOTAL

| a dre__y, bli_s-blue | an allu__ng, gal__y-blue | a lam_e_t, ja__-green | a de_y, mi_t va__ey-green | an effe_v__c__t, cha_p_g_e-green | |
|---|---|---|---|---|---|
| a langu_r__s, rapt__e-blue | an entic__g, cons_e__at__n-blue | a ful_e_t, ber_l-green | a neb_l__s, Ed__-green | a viva__o_s, vir_l__y-brown | |

1.

2.

## LIPS                                           TOTAL

| puf_y lips | be_st__g lips | ox__w lips | tr__t po_t lips | sili___e enha___d | |
|---|---|---|---|---|---|
| pou__ng lips | he__t sh__ed lips | Cup__'s b__ lips | bo__x b__sted | col_a__n enha___d | |

1.

2.

## SWEET LIPS                                     TOTAL

| hon__<br>sweet | stra__e__y<br>sweet | su__r<br>sweet | ch___y<br>sweet | nec___<br>sweet | |
| --- | --- | --- | --- | --- | --- |
| sy__p<br>sweet | sac_ha__ne<br>sweet | su__r<br>ca__y<br>sweet | me___<br>sweet | she___t<br>sweet | |

1.

2.

## PERSONALITY                                   TOTAL

| chee_ful | bu__ly | ele__nt | dem__e | win___g | |
| --- | --- | --- | --- | --- | --- |
| joy_us | bo__cy | lad_l__e | gent_l | inf__ti__s | |

1.

2.

## A SWEET VOICE                                 TOTAL

| soot_ing | su__ry | nect___e | dul__t | mel_d__s | |
| --- | --- | --- | --- | --- | --- |
| son_bi_d<br>sweet | sy__p<br>sweet | sacc___in_ | dulc_m_r<br>sweet | mel__f___s | |

1.

2.

## CLOTHES                                        TOTAL

| gru_gy | vibr__t | chi_ | vogu__h | cosm_p____n | |
| --- | --- | --- | --- | --- | --- |
| got_ic | kid_lt | ret_o | flu__o | na__ | |

1.

2.

# TEACHING CHARACTERISATION

'Writing with Stardust' has been designed to expose the students to the greatest and most effective words possible. This should not stop any educator from being innovative and adding their own expertise to it. In the 'Describing Females' chapter, there is ample room for development of character, personality and more creative ideas. The grids below are left empty in order for an educator to add his/her own stardust to the book. The first grid is based on the book.

## COMPILING A CHARACTER

| personality | clothes | teeth | eyelashes | lips |
|---|---|---|---|---|
| | | | | |
| figure | hair colour | eye colour | nose | voice |
| | | | | |

| | | | | |
|---|---|---|---|---|
| | | | | |
| | | | | |
| | | | | |

| | | | | |
|---|---|---|---|---|
| | | | | |
| | | | | |
| | | | | |

# MALES

## BLOND HAIR

| 1 point | 2 points | 3 points | 4 points | 5 points | TOTAL |
|---------|----------|----------|----------|----------|-------|
| Vik__g-gold | Nordi_-gold | Ar__n-gold | li__s mane-gold | Ach____s-gold | |
| Hercu_es-gold | Scand__a__an-gold | Teu_o__c-gold | mot__r lo_e-gold | A_o__o-gold | |

1.

2.

## SHORT HAIR                                                 TOTAL

| a cre_ cut | a Moh__an | a mar__e cut | a ra___'s edge cut | a bal_ pa__ | |
|------------|-----------|--------------|--------------------|-------------|--|
| clo_e cro__ed | a roo__er cut | a mil___ry cut | a bu__ cut | a chr__e do__ | |

1.

2.

## EYEBROWS                                                  TOTAL

| bus_y | sic__e shaped | cres__nt-o_-m__n | bee__e black | fi__wo_s__p__r-black | |
|-------|---------------|------------------|--------------|---------------------|--|
| bris__y | scy__e shaped | eq__no_-black | hir__te | Ha__s-black | |

1.

2.

## NOSE                                                      TOTAL

| a falc_n's nose | a Ro_an nose | a patr__ian nose | a rapt__'s nose | a lor__y nose | |
|-----------------|--------------|------------------|-----------------|---------------|--|
| a hawk_sh nose | an imp__ial nose | an imper___s nose | an aq__in_ nose | a kin__y nose | |

1.

2.

## CHEEKBONES                                    TOTAL

| do_ed | hal_-dom_ | ar__ed | pin___d-i_ | co_c_e | |
|---|---|---|---|---|---|
| defi_ed | hal_-m__n | ang__ar | pr_mi___t | mo__t__n pe_k | |

1.

2.

## JAW                                           TOTAL

| a concr_te jaw | a cr__gy jaw | a fl__ty jaw | a gr__te jaw | an ada_a_t__e jaw | |
|---|---|---|---|---|---|
| a lan_ern jaw | an oa__n jaw | a ma__le jaw | a bas__t jaw | an obs__ia_ jaw | |

1.

2.

## SHOULDERS                                      TOTAL

| Atl_s shoulders | taur_ne shoulders | sim__n shoulders | Colo___s shoulders | can__n rid__ shoulders | |
|---|---|---|---|---|---|
| a Tit_n's shoulders | a wrest__r's shoulders | Sa__on shoulders | Cori____an shoulders | o_yo_e shoulders | |

1.

2.

## STRENGTH · TOTAL

| | | | | | |
|---|---|---|---|---|---|
| a glad__to_'s bice_s | a goli__h's body | a lev__t_a_'s body | a Spa_t__'s mu__les | a gy_ to_ed phys___e | |
| a stron_m_n's shoulders | a Gre__ go_'s body | Po_e_e fo__ar_s | Schwa_z_e__er mu__les | a gy_ ho_ed phys___e | |

1.

2.

## MASCULINITY · TOTAL

| | | | | | |
|---|---|---|---|---|---|
| dis_y | bra__y | ma__y | hu__y | ha_e and he___y | |
| das_ing | bur_y | str___ing | han___e | he__ from roc_ | |

1.

2.

## MOVEMENT · TOTAL

| | | | | | |
|---|---|---|---|---|---|
| a ca_ like grace | a ti__r like trea_ | an ath___c grace | a li__-like po__r | a fel__e gr__e | |
| a le_pard like grace | su_e-foo__d purp__e | a bal_e__c grace | a le__in_ poi_e | like a pa__h__in slo_-m_ | |

1.

2.

# 20 BASIC ESSAY TITLES

When students get to a certain level of advancement, it is a delight to see them cope with difficult essay titles. For the purposes of descriptive writing, sometimes it is better just to leave the story evolve itself. Underneath are listed some basic titles for students. A teacher or parent may want to make them more confined. Another good idea is to start the story with three or four sentences and see how the student can develop it. In all cases, the essay should be pre-planned. Page 74 has some useful tips on what is expected of a student when he/she is attempting an essay.

1. Rivers and Streams: **Walking by the river.**

2. Mountains: **My mountain disaster.**

3. The Beach: **My summer holidays.**

4. Waterfalls: **My paradise island waterfall.**

5. The Forest: **The enchanted forest.**

6. Lakes: **The becalmed lake.**

7. Spring: **Spring is here!**

8. Summer: **A summer adventure.**

9. Autumn: **Autumn news.**

10. Winter: **Christmas day.**

11. Describing Monsters: **My monster story.**

12. The Desert: **Lost in the desert.**

13. Describing Battle Scenes: **The day I died.**

14. The Mist: Rain: A Flood River: **Alone in the mist.**

15. Thunder and Lightning: **The worst day of my life.**

16. The Dark Forest: **The Grimm Forest.**

17. Describing Females: **My favourite film star or musician.**

18. Describing Females: **Abandoned in the Arctic.**

19. Describing Males: **My favourite sportsman.**

20. Describing Males: **The day we lost the final.**

# MALES

## BEARDS

| 1 Point | 2 Points | 3 Points | 4 Points | 5 Points | TOTAL |
|---------|----------|----------|----------|----------|-------|
| a goa_ee | a spa_e sha_ed beard | an A_e Lin_o_n beard | a Capt__n Ah_b beard | a Mo__s beard | |
| a gal_ay | a devi_'s for_ beard | a Vand__e beard | a Socr___c beard | a Meth__e__h beard | |

1.

2.

## MOUSTACHES

| | | | | | TOTAL |
|---------|----------|----------|----------|----------|-------|
| a bu_hy moustache | a pen__l thin moustache | a too__br__h moustache | a hand__ba_ moustache | a Za_a_a moustache | |
| a bris_ly moustache | a mili_ary moustache | a smi_ | a wal__s moustache | a D'Art__n_n moustache | |

1.

2.

## STUBBLE

| | | | | | TOTAL |
|---------|----------|----------|----------|----------|-------|
| da_k stubble | gra__y stubble | san_-rou_h stubble | mo_n__g sha__w | a rim_ of gre_ | |
| peppe_ed stubble | gri_y stubble | des___er stubble | fi__o' cl__k sh__w | sa__a__ p___er stubble | |

1.

2.

## BLUE EYES · TOTAL

| sea-ro_er blue | no_ad-blue | voy__er-blue | sea__rer-blue | trai__laz_r-blue | |
|---|---|---|---|---|---|
| Raspu__n-blue | naut__al-blue | mar__er-blue | way__rer-blue | wand__lu__-blue | |

1.

2.

## DIFFERENT EYE COLOURS · TOTAL

| hypno_ic, melt wa_er-blue | scorc__ng, smara__ine-green | begu___ng, tur__o_e-green | enthr___ing, cham____e-brown | ench_t_g, cla_-grey | |
|---|---|---|---|---|---|
| mesmeri_ing, empyr_an-blue | irid__cent, malac__te-green | bewi__h_g, tourm___ne-green | entra____g, mol__n-brown | enrap_____g, loa_-grey | |

1.

2.

## SHAPE OF EYES · TOTAL

| do_ shaped | sau__r shaped | or_ round | l__ar shaped | m__n shaped | |
|---|---|---|---|---|---|
| alm_nd shaped | Sat__n shaped | opa_ round | s_oe shaped | mi__po__ round | |

1.

2.

## ARCHAIC WORDS FOR EYES · TOTAL

| a-da__le with wonde_ | a-fl___er with cur___ity | a-gl__m with del__t | a-g__w with l__e | a-s_a__e with mi__h | |
|---|---|---|---|---|---|
| a-f_re with pass__n | a-fl__h with tri__ph | a-gli__er with int___st | a-l__t with j__ | a-tw__le with the joi_d_ vi_re | |

1.

2.

## PERSONALITY                                          TOTAL

| das_ing | de_il-may-c__e | viv___ous | fla_b___nt | bucc____r__g | |
|---|---|---|---|---|---|
| advent_rous | der__ng-d_ | greg_r___s | deb__a_r | swas__u__i_g | |

1.

2.

## VOICE                                          TOTAL

| a de_p voice | a ba_s voice | a fo_h_rn voice | a rum___ng voice | a stent____n voice | |
|---|---|---|---|---|---|
| a boo__ng voice | a tro__one voice | a volc___c voice | like bot__ed thu___r | a gr_t-and-g___y voice | |

1.

2.

## CLOTHES                                          TOTAL

| sna_zy clothes | nat_y clothes | ga_yea_ clothes | rak__h clothes | tw__ clothes | |
|---|---|---|---|---|---|
| rit_y clothes | nif_y clothes | swan_y clothes | raf__h clothes | Mi_i V__e clothes | |

1.

2.

# GRADING AN ESSAY

Grading essays is always more enjoyable for a parent or teacher when it is peer corrected first. The golden rule is to let the students critique each other for mistakes while the educator acts as the guiding hand, providing structure and encouragement. In this way, the student should not become disillusioned or suffer self-esteem problems. All students should be encouraged to read out their work, preferably in front of their peers. All the positive aspects of the work should be listed on a pad as they are reading. What was the best image, the best phrase etc? Their friends or classmates should then assess the grammar, punctuation etc. before it is presented for correction. When it has been corrected by the teacher, it should then be redrafted by the student. Underneath are a basic and a more detailed grid for students and teachers.

# PEER CORRECTING

| STRUCTURE | 20% |
|-----------|-----|
| PLOT | 20% |
| CREATIVITY | 20% |
| ATMOSPHERE | 20% |
| MECHANICS | 20% |

**TEACHER CORRECTING: 5 POINTS PER SQUARE=100%**

| STRUCTURE | Using different narrative 'voices' or styles. | Paragraph structure clear and organised. | The sequence of ideas should be pre-planned. | There should be a flow to the story. |
|---|---|---|---|---|
| PLOT | A good 'hook' sentence. | The reader should be engaged from start to finish. | Has 'flashback' or 'stream-of-thought' been used? | There should be a twist at the end and a good 'unhook' sentence. |
| CREATIVITY | Using 'pulse' words for greater impact. | Unique ideas and original phraseology. | The story should contain memorable characters. | A range of devices should be used: metaphors, assonance etc. |
| ATMOSPHERE | Catapulting the reader into your world. | Using plenty of colours and sounds. | It should elicit a personal response from the reader: joy, anger, outrage etc. | Are 'zoom narration' and 'laser-beam attention to detail' present? |
| MECHANICS | The syntax should be varied but never too long. | The grammar should be free of slang terms. | The spellings should always be peer corrected first. | The punctuation should be peer corrected first. |

## SPRING GREENS AND BLUES

| 30 basic blues | 30 advanced blues | 30 basic greens | 30 advanced greens |
|---|---|---|---|
| alpine-blue | aquamarine-blue | Amazon-green | aphid-green |
| aquarium-blue | Arcadian-blue | carnival-green | baize-green |
| astral-blue | Atlantis-blue | celery-green | beryl-green |
| bilberry-blue | aurora Australis | Eden-green | carousel-green |
| brochure-blue | aurora borealis | fern-green | chartreuse-green |
| butterfly-blue | Babylon-blue | forest-green | chlorophyll-green |
| chemical-blue | bliss-blue | garnish-green | cyan-green |
| cocktail-blue | celestial-blue | grape-green | enchantment-green |
| cosmic-blue | cerulean-blue | glade-green | fairyland-green |
| crystal-blue | constellation-blue | jade-green | fairytale-green |
| dragonfly-blue | divine-blue | juicy-green | forester-green |
| duck-egg blue | Empyrean-blue | lake-green | garland-green |
| electric-blue | fantasy-blue | marble-green | jasper-green |
| gasflame-blue | firmament-blue | meadow-green | Jerusalem-green |
| gemstone-blue | galaxy-blue | milky-green | lapis lazuli-green |
| glacier-blue | halogen-blue | mint-green | luscious-green |
| icemint-blue | nirvana-blue | moss-green | malachite-green |
| Jesus-blue | nitrous-blue | pea-green | mist valley-green |
| jewel-blue | peacock-blue | peppermint-green | paradise-green |
| kingfisher-blue | pellucid-blue | pinemint-green | pristine-green |
| lagoon-blue | Prussian-blue | postcard-green | sacred-green |
| luminous-blue | rapture-blue | reed-green | storybook-green |
| neon-blue | riparian-blue | sage-green | tourmaline-green |
| plasma-blue | serene-blue | sap-green | utopian-green |
| powder-blue | Siberian-blue | sea-green | verdant-green |
| sapphire-blue | stratospheric-blue | sizzling-green | verbena-green |
| solar-blue | topaz-blue | spring leaf-green | virescent-green |
| teal-blue | ultramarine-blue | velvet-green | willow-green |
| universe-blue | wanderlust-blue | watercress-green | wonderland-green |
| woad-blue | Zeus-blue | woodpine-green | Zion-green |

103

# SUMMER BROWNS AND YELLOWS

| 30 summer browns | | 30 summer yellows | |
|---|---|---|---|
| almond-brown | | buttercup-yellow | |
| autumn-brown | | canary-yellow | |
| bamboo-brown | | citrus-yellow | |
| bark-brown | | corn-yellow | |
| beer-brown | animal | daffodil-yellow | |
| biscuit-brown | | gamboge-yellow | gum resin |
| bog-brown | wet place | gold seam-yellow | |
| caramel-brown | | gold vein-yellow | |
| chestnut-brown | | honeycomb-yellow | |
| cinnamon-brown | | lemon-yellow | |
| coconut-brown | | lightning-yellow | |
| conker-brown | slang | marigold-yellow | |
| copper-brown | | melon-yellow | |
| desert-brown | | moon beam-yellow | |
| fawn-brown | animal | moon flame-yellow | |
| kelp-brown | | moon glow-yellow | |
| mahogany-brown | | mustard-yellow | |
| mink-brown | animal | orpiment-yellow | |
| monk-brown | | primrose-yellow | |
| mousy-brown | | saffron-yellow | |
| nut-brown | food | sun flash-yellow | |
| otter-brown | | sunrise-yellow | |
| russet-brown | | sunset-yellow | |
| rust-brown | of metal | syrup-yellow | |
| stew-brown | | treacle-yellow | |
| tannin-brown | | xanthin-yellow | |
| teak-brown | tree | yam-yellow | |
| toast-brown | | yeast-yellow | |
| wafer-brown | | yolk-yellow | |
| walnut-brown | | zestful-yellow | |

## AUTUMN REDS AND GOLDS

| 30  basic reds | 30 advanced reds | 30 glittering golds |
|---|---|---|
| berry-red | balefire-red | Arc-of-Covenant gold |
| blood-red | brazier-red | aureolin-gold |
| bonfire-red | brimstone-red | beeswax-gold |
| claret-red | claret-red | chrome-gold |
| crimson-red | conflagration-red | flaxen-gold |
| devil-red | crematorium-red | fulvous-gold |
| devil flame-red | crucifixion-red | gamboge-gold |
| devil blood-red | damask-red | harp string-gold |
| dragon blood-red | firebrand-red | honeycomb-gold |
| dragon flame-red | firedrake-red | honeydew-gold |
| ember-red | firefly-red | ingot-gold |
| fireball-red | florid-red | lightning-gold |
| firecoal-red | glow-worm-red | lustrous-gold |
| fire core-red | haemoglobin-red | marble-leaf-gold |
| fire flame-red | henna-red | molten-gold |
| fire spark-red | incendiary-red | moon glow-gold |
| hellhound-red | marrow blood-red | moon shimmer-gold |
| holly-red | oxblood-red | nectar-gold |
| inferno-red | phoenix-red | Nordic-gold |
| lava-red | rheumy-red | ore-gold |
| magma-red | rouge-red | star beam-gold |
| mercury-red | rubicund-red | star flash-gold |
| molten-red | rushlight-red | star streak-gold |
| rose-red | sanguine-red | sunset-gold |
| ruby-red | solferino-red | syrup-gold |
| russet-red | sorrel-red | treacle-gold |
| squid-red | stammel-red | Teutonic-gold |
| vampire's eye-red | Titian-red | valkeyrie-gold |
| windfall-red | vermilion-red | waxmelt-gold |
| wine-red | vinaceous-red | as gold as Zeus' eyes |

# WINTER WHITES AND GREYS

| 30 BASIC WHITES | 30 ADVANCED WHITES | 30 GREYS |
|---|---|---|
| angel-white | albata-white | ash-grey |
| Arctic-white | albino-white | argil-grey |
| bleach-white | albumen-white | cenotaph-grey |
| bone-white | aldrin-white | cinder-grey |
| dough-white | archangel-white | clay-grey |
| dove-white | beluga-white | flint-grey |
| fang-white | bleached-bone white | goose-grey |
| flour-white | cadaverous-white | grate-grey |
| goose-white | calcite-white | granite-grey |
| hailstone-white | calico-white | gravel-grey |
| halo-white | crystalline-white | gravestone-grey |
| lice-white | egret-white | grit-grey |
| marble-white | ermine-white | grizzled-grey |
| orb-white | glair-white | hill-mist-grey |
| orchid-white | jasmine-white | iron-grey |
| oyster-white | narwhal-white | lead-grey |
| phantom-white | nimbus-white | loam-grey |
| polar-white | orchid-white | lupine-grey |
| porcelain-white | pasty-white | manacle-grey |
| powder-white | a polar, ice-white | pachyderm-grey |
| putty-white | pristine-white | pumice-grey |
| seashell-white | quicklime-white | sepulchre-grey |
| skull-white | scallop-white | shale-grey |
| snowdrop-white | tallow-white | smoke-grey |
| snowflake-white | truffle-white | spectre-grey |
| swan-white | tuft-cloud-white | tombstone-grey |
| unicorn-white | valkeyrie-white | undead-grey |
| vampire-white | whalebone-white | wayfarer-grey |
| wan-white | whey-white | werewolf-grey |

## BLACKS AND SPARKLING SILVERS

| 30 basic blacks | 30 avanced blacks | 30 sparkling silvers |
|---|---|---|
| abyss-black | apocalypse-black | aluminium-silver |
| basalt-black | Armageddon-black | argent-silver |
| bat-black | Barabbas-black | beryllium-silver |
| cat-black | Beelzebub-black | bubble-silver |
| cave-black | benzene-black | chainmail-silver |
| cellar-black | bitumen-black | chrysalis-silver |
| cobalt-black | blasphemous-black | dew-glint silver |
| cobra-black | carnal-black | diamond-flame silver |
| coral-black | carrion-black | dragon-scale silver |
| corbie-black | cauldron-black | frazil-silver |
| cowl-black          hood | caulk-black | glitter-silver |
| devil's-cloak black | Charon-black | hoarfrost-silver |
| devil's-heart black | cloven-hoof black | ice-silver |
| devil's-soul black | cobalt-black | mere-silver          lake |
| doom-black | cordite-black | moon-glow silver |
| ebony-black | coven-black | nickle-silver |
| gunpowder-black | damask-black | orris-silver |
| kohl-black | damnation-black | platinum-silver |
| mamba-black          snake | gloss-black | salmon-silver |
| maw-black | heathen-black | sardine-silver |
| midnight-black | jewel-black | sea-crest silver |
| raven-black | obsidian-black | slipper-of-fairy silver |
| panther-black | pagan-black | starspark-silver |
| sabre-black | pentacostal-black | skyline-silver |
| scarecrow-black | profane-black | spangle-silver |
| tar-black | Stygian-black | supernova-silver |
| thundercloud-black | succubus-black | surf-silver |
| toad-black | vulcanite-black | sylvan-silver |
| velvet-black | warlock-black | whirlpool-silver |
| witch-soul black | warmonger-black | yttrium-silver |

# PURPLES ORANGES AND PINKS

| 20 purples | 20 oranges | 20 pinks |
|---|---|---|
| amethyst-purple | amber-orange | blossom-pink |
| bird-of-paradise purple | aureolin-orange | a blushing, pilgrim-pink |
| bishop's mitre-purple | blazing-orange | calamine-pink |
| gridelin-purple | boiling-orange | candyfloss-pink |
| heather-purple | broiling-orange | cerise-pink |
| indigo-purple | burning-orange | dawn-pink |
| juniper-purple | ember-orange | diamond-pink |
| lavender-purple | glowing-orange | dusky-pink |
| lilac-purple | feverish-orange | flamingo-pink |
| magenta-purple | fiery-orange | flesh-pink |
| mauve-purple | hot-orange | fuchsia-pink |
| monarchy-purple | nacarat-orange | peony-pink |
| mulberry-purple | ochre-orange | petal-pink |
| orpine-purple | scorching-orange | prawn-pink |
| peacock-purple | smouldering-orange | rose-pink |
| plum-purple | sunset-orange | rosepetal-pink |
| prune-purple | sweltering-orange | salmon-pink |
| royal-purple | tangerine-orange | sorbet-pink |
| Tyrian-purple | tiger stripe-orange | sunrise-pink |
| violet-purple | vulpine-orange | orchid-pink |

# Author's Bio

Liam O' Flynn has been an English teacher in St. Aidan's Community College in Cork for the past twenty years. In that time, he has taught to a whole range of abilities and ages with considerable success. He is 43 years of age and single but in a long term relationship. A resident of Clonmel, he is a dedicated member of the writers' group there.

Liam's interests are: descriptive writing, nature walks, golf and fishing. He keeps a log of the birds who visit his garden, as one does, and has reached the grand total of 32 species. To the peregrine falcon and the sparrow hawk, species number 31 and 32, he has only two words: go away. His next book shall be an adventure/fantasy book for teenagers.

Thanks to Attracta, Brigid, Dave, Mary, Michael, Paddy and Tony from the writers' group. Each of you is talented, gracious and special and I treasure the Tuesday nights with you all.

Thanks to Adrian, Tony and Frank. You know why.

Special thanks also to Bernard, Danielle and Pat, lifeboats on a stormy sea.

Thanks to Davey K; a friend in need is a friend indeed.

To my wonderful girlfriend Lillian, my brothers Alan, Derek and Ray, my sister Gemma, my father Liam and mother Phil and my great friends Fergal, Rossi and Paul; cheers for the support everyone. You are always in my thoughts.

Made in the USA
San Bernardino, CA
24 February 2017